Student Book and CD-ROM

Course Companion GCSE Mathematics

Foundation Tier
Linear and Modular

Fiona Mapp
Gillian Rich

A PEARSON COMPANY

Edexcel
190 High Holborn
London WC1V 7BH
UK

ISBN-10 1-84690-161-8 **ISBN-13** 978-1-84690-161-4

Printed and bound in Great Britain by Scotprint, Haddington
Prepared for Edexcel by Starfish Design, Editorial and Project Management Ltd
Project management by Heather Morris
Illustrated by Peters and Zabransky Ltd

The publisher's policy is to use paper manufactured from sustainable forests.

Contents

Guide to the GCSE Mathematics examination (linear and modular)

The GCSE Mathematics examination can be sat at two tiers, Higher and Foundation, and with a choice of two specifications, one modular and one linear. For example, you may be doing a Foundation level GCSE which is examined at the end of the two years – i.e. the linear course. The modular examinations begin in March 2007 and the linear ones are in June 2008.

GCSE Mathematics coursework

Assessment objective 1 (AO1)

AO1 is known as Using and Applying Mathematics and assessed in the coursework element of GCSE Mathematics. It is also assessed in one of the examination papers. Depending on the examination board that your school is using, AO1 is assessed using one of several methods. These are as follows:

- At least one task which demonstrates ability to use and apply mathematics. These tasks can be practical or investigational and are marked by the school. They count for 10% of the final mark.
- At least one task which demonstrates ability to use and apply mathematics. These tasks can be practical or investigational and are marked by the exam board. They count for 10% of the final mark.

Assessment objective 4 (AO4)

AO4 is known as Handling Data. You are required to produce a project, using knowledge skills and understanding in Handling Data. The project forms part of your coursework assessment and accounts for 10% of the final mark. This project can also be used for a Statistics GCSE.

Note

For students starting their GCSE course in, or after, September 2007, there will be no coursework element. As a result the weightings of the remaining assessment components will change.

Linear GCSE

A linear GCSE is a GCSE where all the content of the syllabus is covered over a two-year period and then assessed with examinations in the June of the second year. There will be two parallel examination papers, on different days, each counting for 40% of the final mark.

Foundation Tier	Paper 1	Non-calculator	1 hour 30 minutes
Foundation Tier	Paper 2	With calculator	1 hour 30 minutes
Higher Tier	Paper 1	Non-calculator	1 hour 45 minutes
Higher Tier	Paper 2	With calculator	1 hour 45 minutes

Modular GCSE

A modular GCSE is where the content of the specification is broken down into units. Units 2 and 3 are assessed in November, March or June. Examinations for Unit 4 are available only in June and November. The weighting of the units is as follows.

Unit 1 – Coursework, which accounts for 20% of the final mark, assessed in June and November only.

Units	**Unit 2** **Two equal sections**	**Unit 3** **Two equal sections**	**Unit 4** **Two parallel terminal examination papers**	
	Section A with calculator **Section B non-calculator**	**Section A with calculator** **Section B non-calculator**	**Non-calculator paper**	**With calculator paper**
Weighting	10% weighting	20% weighting	25% weighting	25% weighting
Foundation Tier	Paper 8 40 minutes	Paper 10 1 hour	Paper 12 1 hour	Paper 13 1 hour
Higher Tier	Paper 9 40 minutes	Paper 11 1 hour	Paper 14 1 hour 10 minutes	Paper 15 1 hour 10 minutes

What is needed to be awarded a grade C in Mathematics?

These statements give a general indication of the standards you will need to achieve to obtain a Grade C. Your final grade will depend on how well you have met the assessment objectives overall. Shortcomings in some areas may be balanced by better performance in others.

A grade C candidate must be able to:

- Give reasons, justify and explain solutions to problems.
- When making estimates, round to one significant figure and multiply and divide mentally.
- Solve numerical problems involving multiplication and division using a calculator efficiently.
- Understand the effects of multiplying and dividing by numbers between 0 and 1
- Calculate using ratios and proportional change.
- Find the *n*th term of a sequence.
- Calculate one quantity as a percentage of another
- Multiply two expressions of the form $(x + n)$ and simplify the resulting quadratic expression.
- Solve equations by using trial and improvement.
- Represent inequalities using a number line.
- Form and solve linear equations.
- Manipulate simple algebraic expressions, equations and formulae.
- Draw and use graphs of quadratic functions.
- Solve problems using the angle and symmetry properties of polygons and intersecting and parallel lines.
- Understand and use Pythagoras' theorem in two dimensions.
- Solve problems involving areas and circumferences of a circle.
- Calculate lengths, areas and volumes of shapes and prisms.
- Enlarge shapes by a positive or fractional scale factor.
- Recognise that a measurement given to a nearest whole number may be inaccurate by up to one half of a unit in either direction.
- Understand and use compound measures such as speed.
- Use mathematical instruments to carry out accurate constructions of loci.
- Construct and interpret frequency diagrams with grouped data.
- Specify hypotheses and test them.
- State the modal class and estimate the mean, median and range of a set of grouped data.
- Use frequency distributions and measures of average and range to compare distributions.
- Use relative frequency as an estimate of probability.

1 Introducing number

Key facts

- Each digit in a number has a place value. The size of the number depends on its place value.

Thousands	Hundreds	Tens	Units
4	6	3	5

Four thousand six hundred and thirty five

- Large numbers are often approximated to the nearest ten, hundred and thousand. For example, 63 is approximately 60 as it is nearer to 60 than 70 and 7562 would be 8000 to the nearest thousand.
- Multiples of a number are the result of multiplying that number by a positive whole number. For example, multiples of 6 are 6 12 18 ... etc.
- Factors are whole numbers which divide exactly into another number. For example, the factors of 24 are 1 2 3 4 6 8 12 24
- A prime number is a whole number that only has 2 factors, 1 and itself. 1 is not a prime number. The prime numbers up to 20 are 2 3 5 7 11 13 17 19
- Numbers can be written as a product of their prime factors. Prime factors are factors which are prime numbers. For example, 24 when written as a product of its prime factors, is

$$24 = 2 \times 2 \times 2 \times 3$$

- The Highest Common Factor (HCF) is the largest factor that two numbers have in common. For example, the HCF of 6 and 12 is 6
- The Lowest Common Multiple (LCM) is the lowest number which is a multiple of two numbers. For example, the LCM of 5 and 6 is 30

Definitions

- **Sum** total of 2 or more numbers
- **Difference** subtraction of a small number from a larger number
- **Product** result of multiplying 2 or more numbers together

Examiner's tips

- When carrying out calculations, it is important to check your answer. To check whether a calculation is correct, use the opposite or inverse operation. For example, the opposite of multiplying is dividing and the opposite of addition is subtraction.

Can you answer these questions?

1. Write these numbers in order. Start with the smallest.

   64 72 5462 6384 67 12 209

2. (a) Write 2735 to the nearest ten.

   (b) Write 62 531 to the nearest hundred.

3. A box holds 23 packets of crisps. How many packets of crisps are there in 6 boxes?

4. A box of 24 calculators cost £156 Find the cost of one calculator.

5. Write down the first four multiples of these numbers.

   (a) 7 (b) 12 (c) 4

6. List all the factors of these numbers.

   (a) 8 (b) 12 (c) 28

7. Find the HCF and LCM of these pairs of numbers.

   (a) 12 and 15 (b) 6 and 10 (c) 4 and 12

Look on the CD for more exam practice questions

2 Collecting and recording data

Key facts

- A sample is a group of observations that are representative, random and without bias.
- Unbiased means as fair as possible.
- A questionnaire is a set of questions for collecting primary data.
  Questionnaires should have:

  short, clear questions

  tick (response) boxes covering all possible answers.

  Questionnaires should not have:

  biased or leading questions. For example, 'Don't you agree ...?'

  open-ended questions. For example, 'What do you think ..?'
- Secondary data is data collected by someone else.
- A tally chart is a simple data collection sheet.
- Discrete data has separate values. For example, shoe sizes, where frequency is counted.
- Continuous data has any value, with no gaps. For example, height, which is measured.

Definitions

- **Database** large amounts of information stored in an organised way
- **Frequency** number of observations or events happening

Did you know?

- People used to count by making notches on a tally stick.

Look on the CD for more exam practice questions

Examiner's tips

- When counting frequency of items of data in a tally chart, write each 5th mark across the previous 4 marks. This looks like a 5-bar gate 卌. You can now count in 5s, which is easier than counting 1s and so there is less chance of making a mistake.
- Marks are given for completing tally and frequency columns correctly.

Can you answer these questions?

1. Your school cafeteria decides to do a survey to find out the food pupils prefer. Design a questionnaire for them to use. Include 6 possible lunches.
2. Design a data collection sheet for each question in the questionnaire above. Make up 30 responses and enter them in your sheet.
3. Are the following discrete or continuous data?
   (a) height of flowers in garden
   (b) number of goals scored by teams during one weekend
   (c) weight of tomatoes in a box
   (d) shoe sizes of a year 10 class
4. Why are these questions inappropriate for a questionnaire? Rewrite them.
   (a) How old are you?
   (b) Don't you think that teenagers should go to bed before 9.30pm?
   (c) Do you agree that everyone should read a newspaper every day?

3 Angles 1

Key facts

- There are 3 different types of angle.

  $0° <$ acute angle $< 90°$

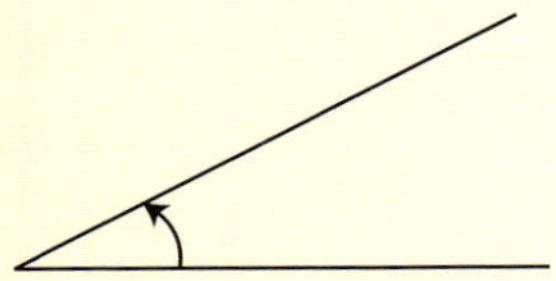

  $90° <$ obtuse angle $< 180°$

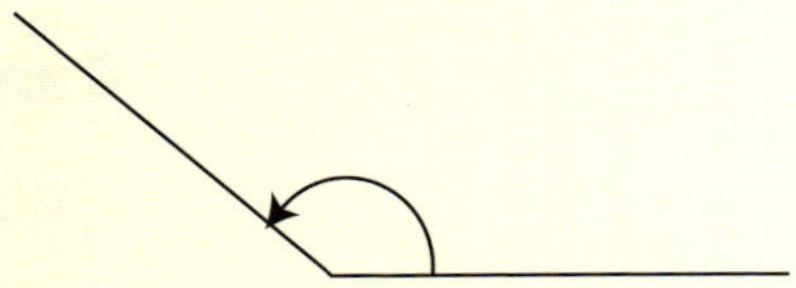

  $180° <$ reflex angle $< 360°$

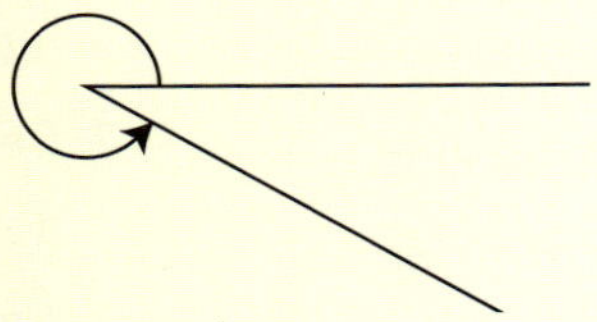

- When a line is perpendicular to another line, they meet at 90° (a right angle).

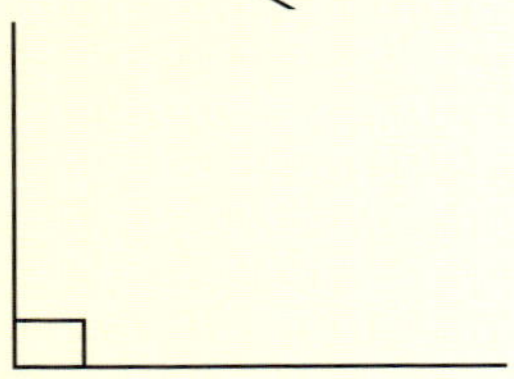

- Angles meeting at a point add up to 360°.

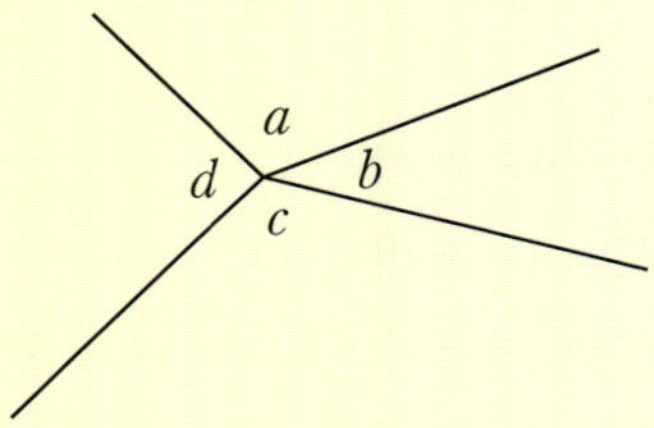

$a + b + c + d = 360°$

- The sum of angles on a straight line is 180°.

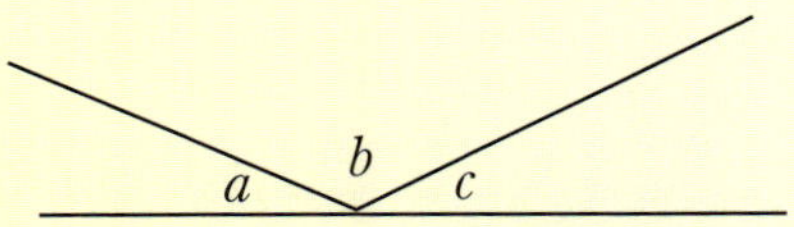

$a + b + c = 180°$

- When straight lines cross, the opposite angles are equal.

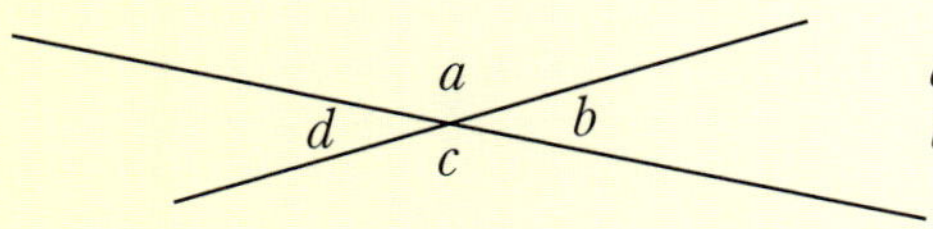

$a = c$
$b = d$

- When a straight line crosses parallel lines, corresponding (c) and alternate angles (a) are formed: $a_1 = a_2$ and $c_1 = c_2$

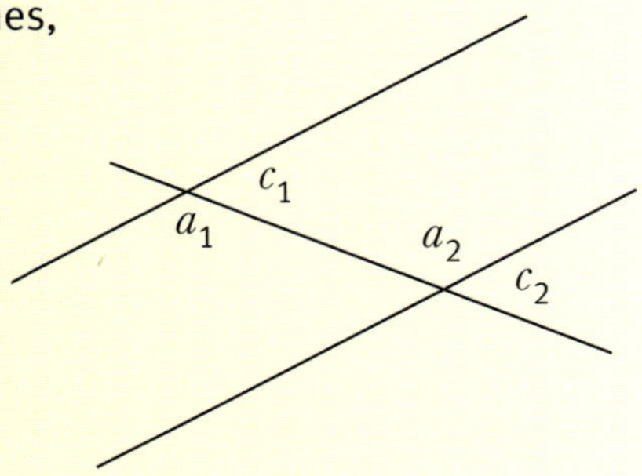

Definitions

- **Parallel** lines always stay the same distance apart and never meet

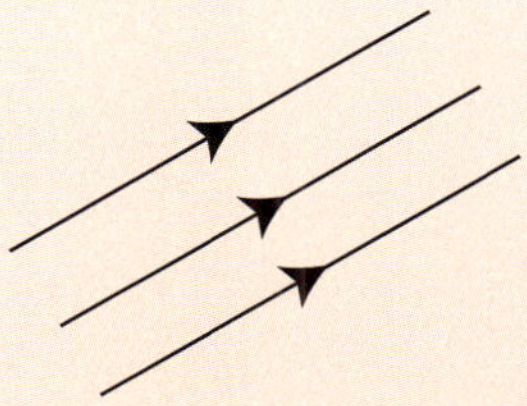

- **Perpendicular** a line at right angles to another line

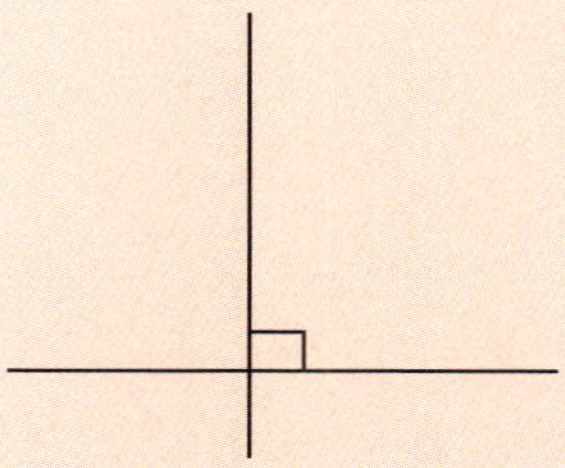

Examiner's tips

- Always use a sharp pencil to draw lines and angles so that you can rub out any mistakes.
- When measuring or drawing angles:
  - place your protractor so that the 0°–180° line is exactly over the base line of your angle and the centre of this line on the corner (vertex) of the angle
  - use the scale that has 0° sitting on the base line.
- When estimating angles:
  - a right angle is easy to spot because it looks like the corner of a page
  - decide if the angle is acute, obtuse or reflex
  - try to picture what a right angle (90°), $\frac{1}{2}$ right angle (45°), $\frac{1}{3}$ right angle (30°) and so on looks like
  - divide the angle into recognisable smaller angles
  - if the angle is reflex, it may be easier to estimate the remaining angle and take it away from 360°.

Can you answer these questions?

1. Estimate these angles.

(a)

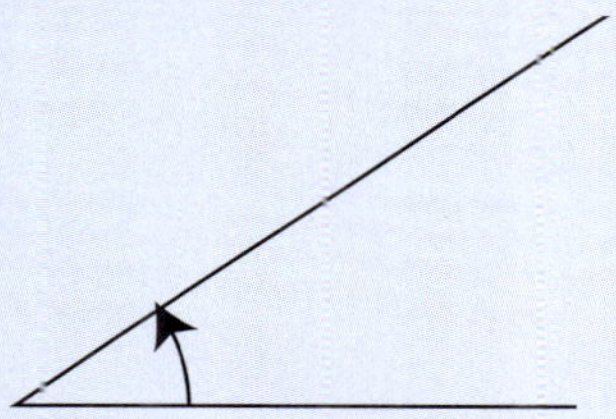

(b)

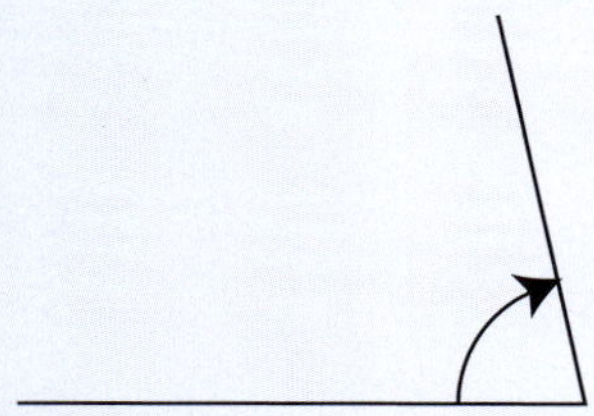

(c)

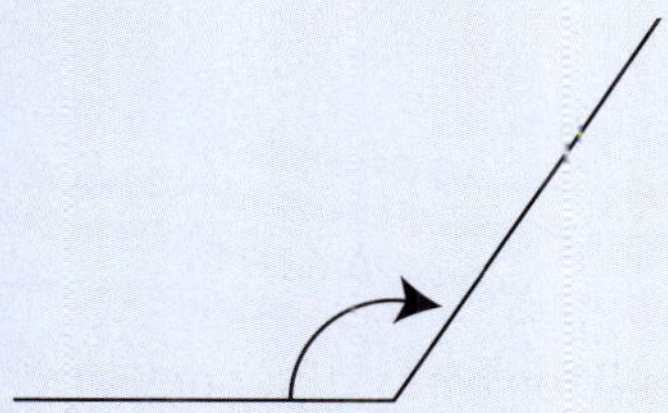

(d)

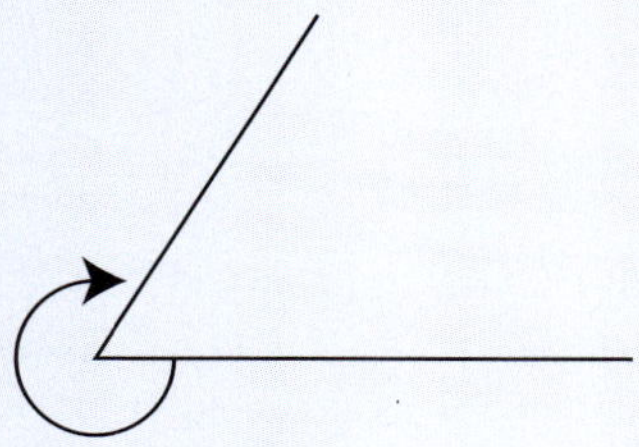

2. Name the type of angle.

(a)

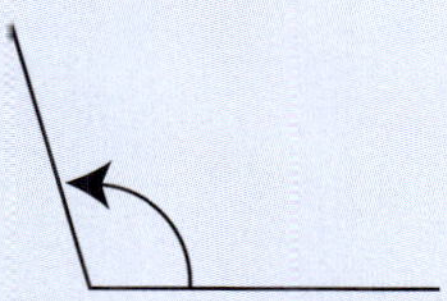

(b)

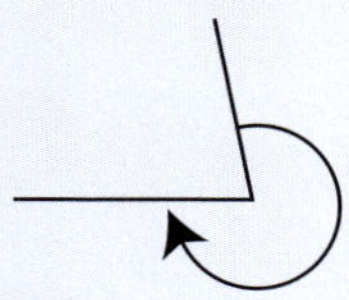

(c)

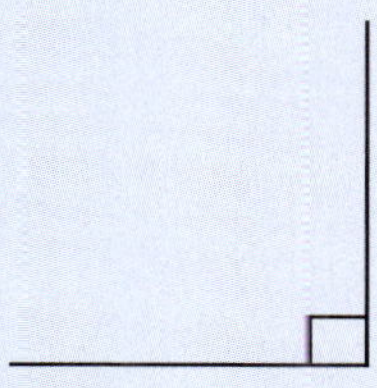

(d)

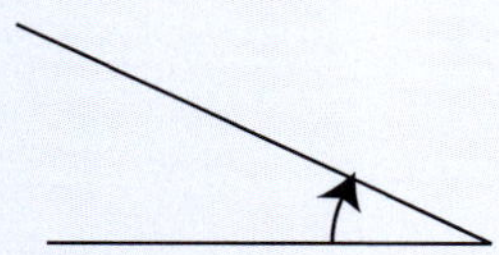

▶ *continued*

3. Calculate the missing angles.

(a)

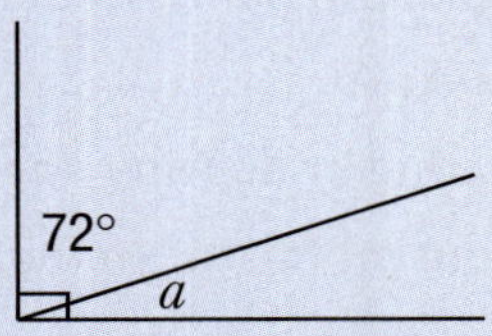

(b)

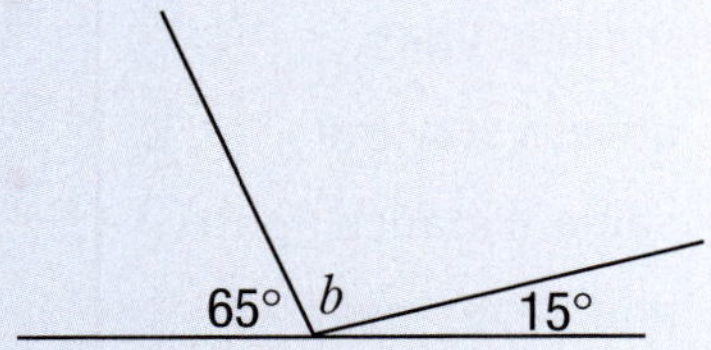

(c)

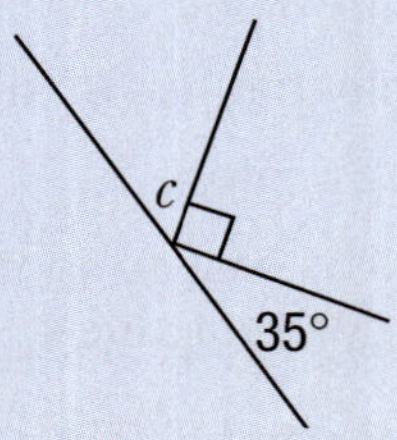

(d)

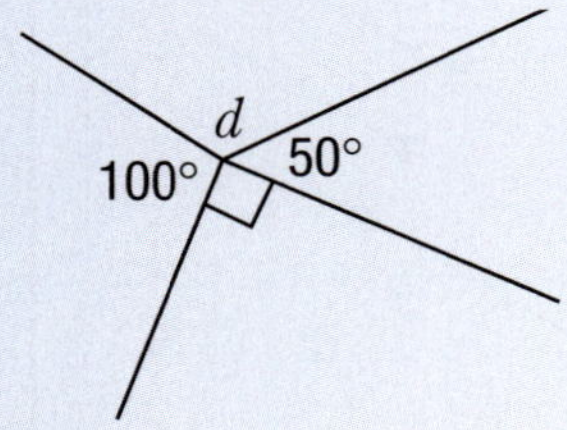

(e)

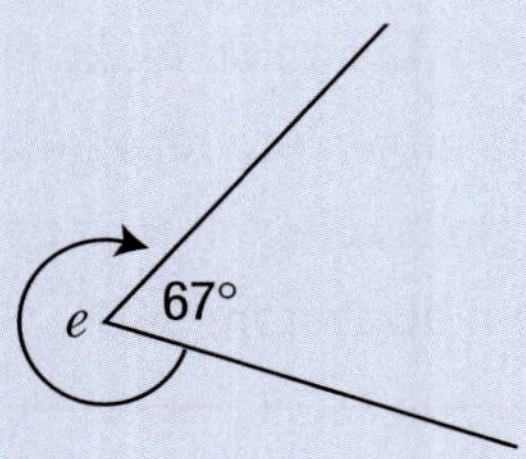

(f)

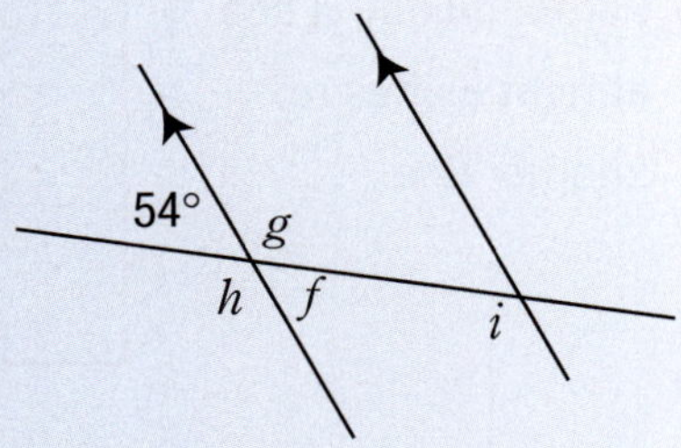

Look on the CD for more exam practice questions

3 Angles 2

Have you ever wondered?

Why are bearings measured from north in a clockwise direction?

Key facts

- Types of triangles:

  equilateral (3 equal sides, 3 equal angles)

  isosceles (2 equal sides with their opposite angles also equal)

  scalene (3 different sides, 3 different angles).

- Angle sum of a triangle = 180°
- Exterior angle of a triangle = sum of 2 opposite interior angles.
- Types of **polygons:**

  quadrilateral (4 sides, angle sum = 360°)

  pentagon (5 sides)

  hexagon (6 sides)

  octagon (8 sides)

  decagon (10 sides).

- Angle sum of a polygon = (number of sides − 2) x 180°

  (find this by drawing diagonals from 1 vertex. For example, if 3 triangles can be drawn, then

  angle sum = 3 × 180° = 540°)

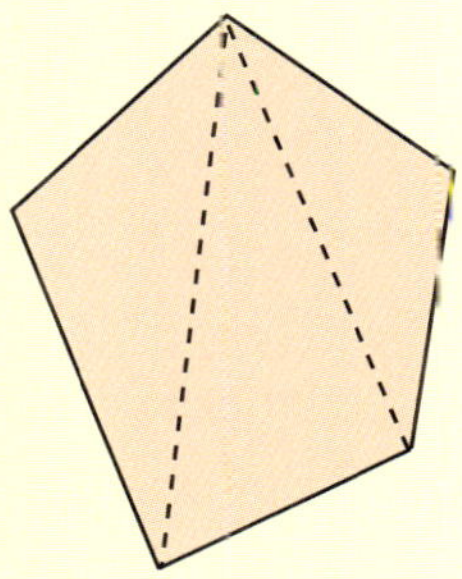

- Exterior angle of a regular polygon = 360° ÷ number of sides.
- Interior angle + Exterior angle = 180°
- A line crossing parallel lines forms:

  equal alternate angles

  equal corresponding angles.

  (See diagram page 12)

Definitions

- **Polygon** 2D shape with many straight lines
- **Bearing** direction of an object, given by 3-figure angle, measured clockwise from the north line

Examiner's tips

- Make diagrams easier to read by marking:
  parallel sides with arrows
  equal sides with short lines.
- Remember to measure **bearings** clockwise from north.
- Marks are given for showing angle calculations. For example, 180° – ?, 360° – ?
- Always give reasons for angle calculation. For example, angles on straight line.

Can you answer these questions?

1. Each of these triangles has an extended side. Find the missing angles.

(a)

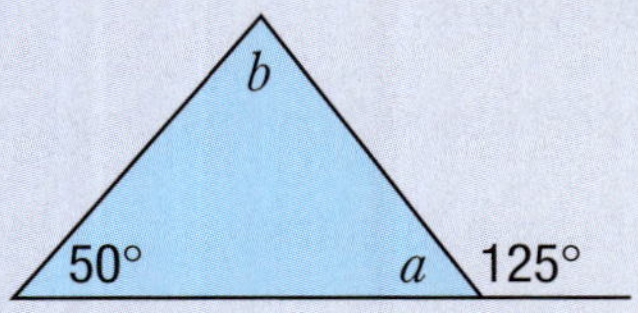

(b)

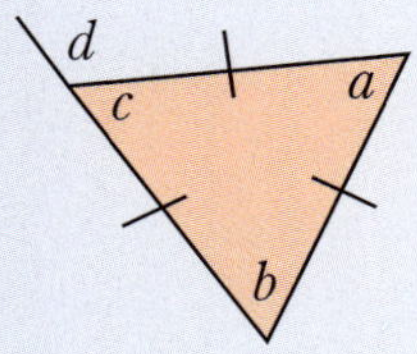

(c)

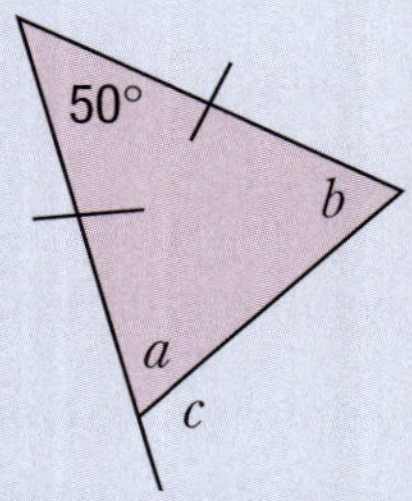

(d)

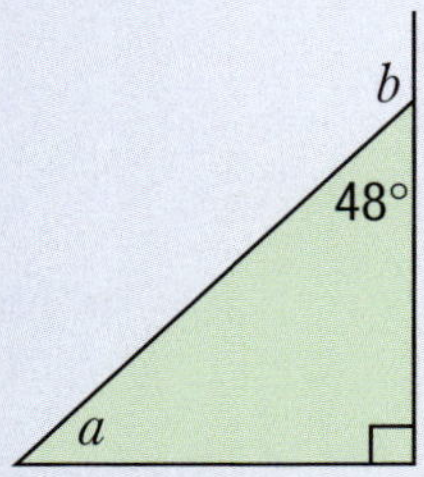

2. Calculate the missing angles.

(a)

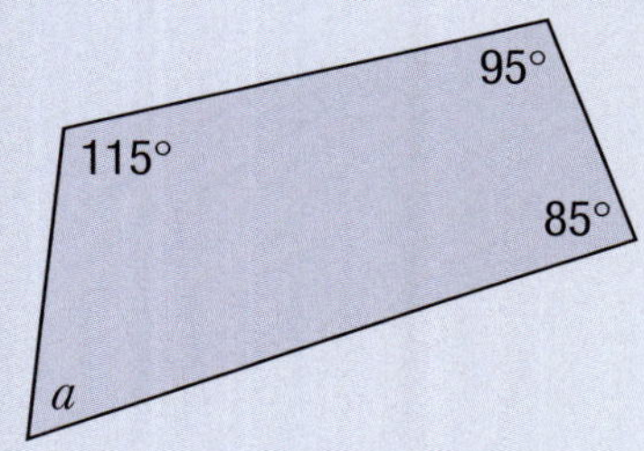

(b)

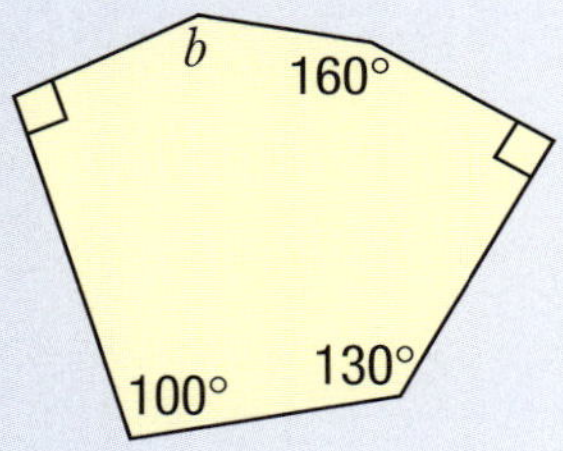

(c)

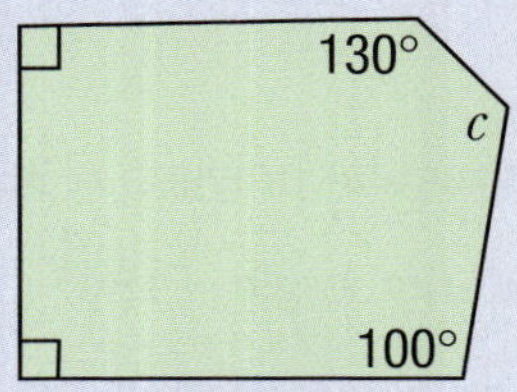

(d)

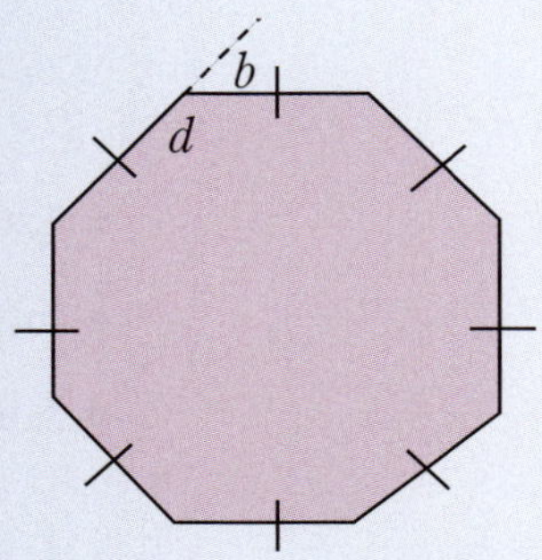

▶ *continued*

Did you know?

- There are 2 North Poles. There is a geographic North Pole and a magnetic North Pole.

(e)

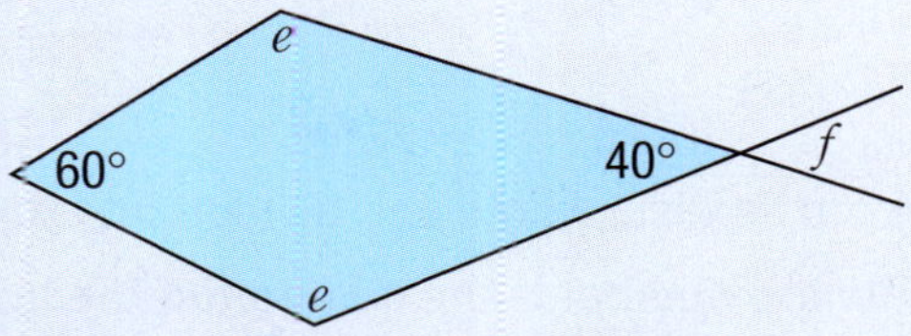

3. Measure the bearings of (a) B from A (b) C from B (c) C from A.

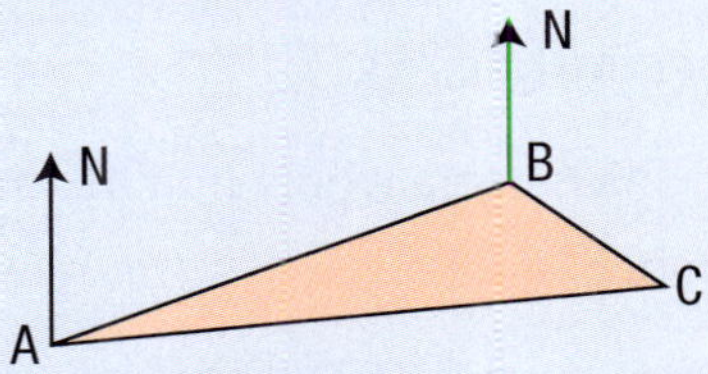

4. Calculate the bearings of (a) B from A (b) C from B (c) A from C.

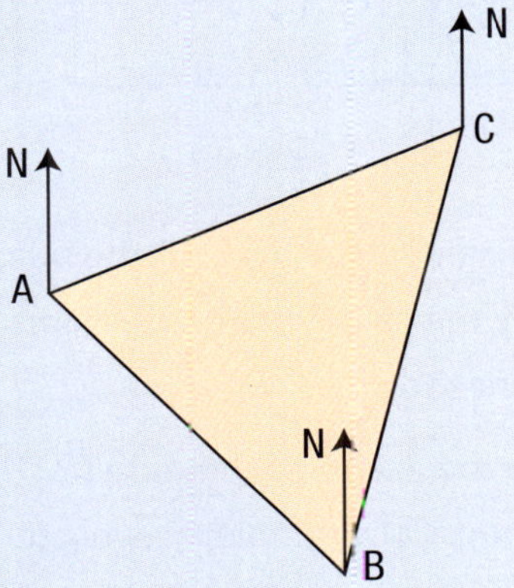

Look on the CD for more exam practice questions

4 Fractions and decimals 1

Key facts

- A fraction is a whole unit divided into equal parts. $\frac{5}{7}$ means 5 parts out of 7 The top number is the **numerator**, the bottom number is the **denominator**.
- If the numerator is smaller than the denominator it is called a proper fraction, e.g. $\frac{5}{9}$ If the numerator is bigger than the denominator it is called an improper fraction, e.g. $\frac{9}{5}$
- A fraction which has a whole number and a fraction, e.g. $2\frac{1}{3}$ is called a mixed number.
- Fractions that have equal values are called equivalent fractions, e.g. $\frac{1}{2} = \frac{2}{4}$

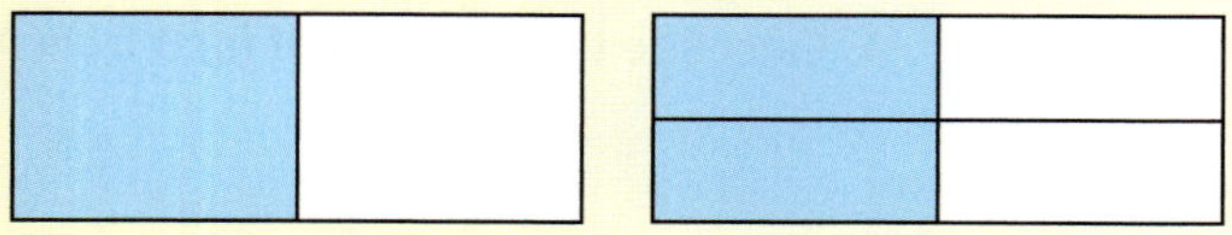

$\frac{1}{2}$ $\frac{2}{4}$

- A fraction can be simplified if the numerator and the denominator can be divided by the same number. This process is called cancelling. For example, $\frac{20}{50}$ simplifies to $\frac{2}{5}$.
- When you are asked to compare fractions, write them with a common denominator. For example, $\frac{2}{3}$ is bigger than $\frac{4}{9}$ since $\frac{2}{3} = \frac{6}{9}$.
- Decimals are used for parts of a number which are less than 1 A decimal point is used to separate whole number columns from fractional columns.

Thousands	Hundreds	Tens	Units		Tenths	Hundredths	Thousandths
7	6	5	4	.	3	2	1

↑ Decimal point

The column headings tell us the place value of each figure. The 2 has a value of two hundredths.

- When converting decimals to fractions, use the place values of the figures.

  For example, $0.37 = \frac{3}{10} + \frac{7}{100} = \frac{37}{100}$
- When converting fractions to decimals, divide the numerator by the denominator.

  For example, $\frac{4}{5} = 4 \div 5 = 0.8$
- A decimal that recurs is shown by placing a dot over the numbers that repeat. For example, 0.252525 ... = $0.\dot{2}\dot{5}$

Worked example

Write the numbers 4.3   4.29   4.62   4.06   4.37 in order of size. Start with the smallest.

Solution

Write the numbers in a table using column headings to show the value of each figure. Compare the numbers in each column.

Units	.	Tenths	Hundredths
4	.	3	0
4	.	2	9
4	.	6	2
4	.	0	6
4	.	3	7

So the answer is 4.06   4.29   4.3   4.37   4.62

Definitions

- **Numerator** number above the line in a fraction
- **Denominator** number below the line in a fraction

Examiner's tips

- Questions which involve fractions often ask you to 'give your answer in its simplest form'. This means cancel down the fraction. For example, $\frac{6}{9}$ cancels to $\frac{2}{3}$

Can you answer these questions?

1. There are 64 books on a shelf. 24 of the books are fiction and the rest are non-fiction. Write down the fraction of the books that are non-fiction. Give your answer in its simplest form.
2. Fill in the missing number to make these fractions equivalent.
   (a) $\frac{2}{3} = \frac{?}{9}$ (b) $\frac{6}{7} = \frac{?}{21}$ (c) $\frac{10}{15} = \frac{?}{3}$
3. Write these fractions in order of size. Start with the smallest.
   $\frac{1}{6}$ $\frac{7}{12}$ $\frac{5}{24}$
4. Write down the value of the 3 in the number 4.23
5. Write the numbers 6.4   6.72   6.05   6.57   6.572 in order of size. Write the smallest first.
6. Write 2.69 as a fraction.
7. Write $\frac{2}{9}$ as a decimal.

Look on the CD for more exam practice questions

5 Two-dimensional shapes

Key facts

- A line (axis) of **symmetry** or mirror line divides a shape into 2 equal halves.
- Line symmetry is also known as reflection symmetry.
- **2-D** shape: rotational symmetry is the number of positions the shape can take, when rotated, and still look the same. Number of positions = order of rotational symmetry.
- To draw a triangle: draw base line using ruler; set compasses to length of side; with point on 1 end of line, draw arc; repeat with other side; draw line from each end of line to point where arcs cross. Use protractor to measure angles if necessary.
- To draw a quadrilateral: follow similar method as for a triangle, working round shape.
- To draw a circle: set compasses to radius length; make sure point is firmly in paper and there is enough room to draw.
- Congruent shapes have equal sides and equal angles.
- All regular polygons have line symmetry, but they do not all have rotational symmetry.
- Parts of a circle

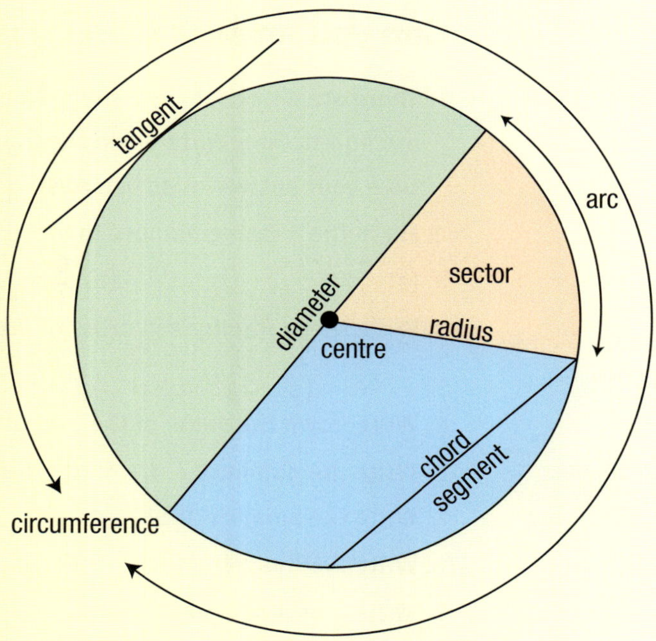

- 2-D shapes tessellate if the shapes can be fitted together and a pattern can be repeated without gaps.

Definitions

- **2-D** two dimensional – has length and breadth but no depth
- **Symmetry** stays the same when reflected or rotated

Did you know?

- You can work out the number of sides of a polygon from its name.
  For example,
  quad means 4
  penta means 5
  hexa means 6

Look on the CD for more exam practice questions

Examiner's tips

- Always draw a rough sketch before starting an accurate construction.
- You will need a sharp pencil, ruler and compasses. Sometimes you may use a protractor.
- Never rub out arcs or any other construction lines.
- Full marks are only given when working is shown as well as answer, e.g. $\pi \times d = \pi d$

Can you answer these questions?

1. Do these letters have line or rotational symmetry? If so, draw in the lines or give the order of rotational symmetry.

   A B P S

2. (a) Draw triangle XYZ where XY = 7 cm, YZ = 8 cm, ZX = 9 cm. Measure ∠X.

   (b) Draw a regular pentagon with side 3 cm. Measure any interior angle.

3. Look at these 7 shapes. There are 3 pairs of congruent shapes. Which are they?

4. Draw a circle of radius 3 cm. Label these:

   diameter, arc, chord, tangent, sector, segment

5. Draw a 6-sided shape and tessellate it on squared paper.

6 Directed numbers

Key facts

- Directed numbers may be positive or negative. Positive numbers are above zero, negative numbers are below zero.

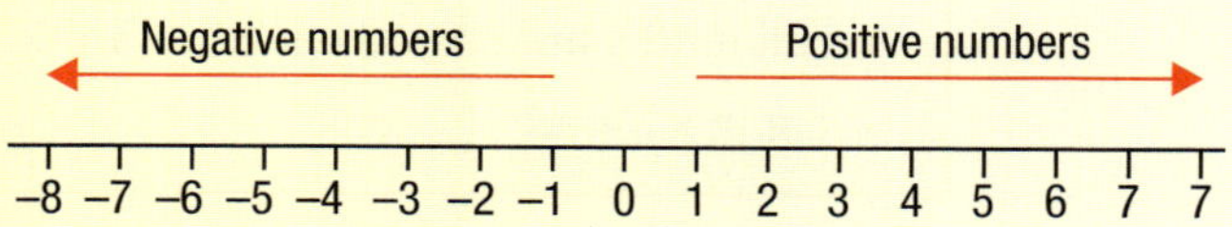

- Subtracting a positive number is the same as adding the negative number. For example,

  $6 - (+3) = 3$

  $6 + (-3) = 3$

- Subtracting a negative number is the same as adding the positive number. For example,

  $7 - (-3) = 10$

  $7 + (+3) = 10$

- When multiplying or dividing directed numbers:

  two like signs (both + or both –) give a positive sign

  two unlike signs (one + and the other –) give a negative sign.

  These tables will help you remember.

+	×	+	=	+
+	×	–	=	–
–	×	+	=	–
–	×	–	=	+

+	÷	+	=	+
+	÷	–	=	–
–	÷	+	=	–
–	÷	–	=	+

  The results are the same for multiplying and dividing.

- Basic calculators have a 'change sign' key. +/–

- Scientific calculators have a negative sign shown by (–)

Examiner's tips

- When calculating with directed numbers drawing a number line can help you visualise the problem. For example, $-3 - 4 = -7$

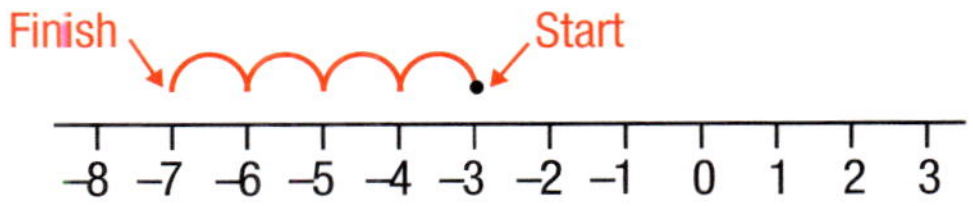

Can you answer these questions?

1. Put these temperatures in order. Start with the lowest temperature.

   −6 °C   4 °C   −2 °C   0 °C   7 °C   −10 °C

2. On Saturday the temperature was 7 °C. By Tuesday, the temperature had fallen by 9 °C. Find the temperature on Tuesday.

3. Work out

   (a) $(-3) + (-2)$ (b) $(-6) - (-3)$ (c) $(-2) + (-3)$

   (d) $-6 - (-5)$ (e) $(-4) + (3)$ (f) $(-6) + (-2)$

4. Work out

   (a) $2 \times (-4)$ (b) $(-3) \times (-4)$ (c) $12 \div (-2)$

   (d) $-6 \div (-2)$ (e) $40 \div (-2)$ (f) $(-6) \times (-4)$

5. Using a calculator work out the answer to

   $$\frac{(-6.9) + (3.2)}{-7.4}$$

Look on the CD for more exam practice questions

7 Decimals 2

Key facts

- When adding or subtracting decimals, line up the decimal points first. For example, 2.72 + 6.093

$$\begin{array}{r} 2.72 \\ +\ 6.093 \\ \hline 8.813 \\ \hline \end{array}$$

- To multiply a decimal by 10, move the figures one place to the left. For example, $6.42 \times 10 = 64.2$
- To multiply a decimal by 100, move the figures two places to the left. For example, $7.293 \times 100 = 729.3$
- To multiply a decimal by 1000, move the figures three places to the left. For example, $62.593 = 62\,593$
- To divide a decimal by 10, move the figures one place to the right. For example, $63.9 \div 10 = 6.39$
- To divide a decimal by 100, move the figures two places to the right. For example, $50.6 \div 100 = 0.506$
- To divide a decimal by 1000, move the figures three places to the right. For example, $72.6 \div 1000 = 0.0726$
- To divide a number by a decimal, multiply both the number and the decimal by a power of 10 to make the decimal a whole number. For example,

$$\frac{64}{0.2} \overset{\times 10}{=} \frac{640}{2} = 320$$

(numerator × 10, denominator × 10)

- The number 7.493 has 3 decimal places, because there are three numbers after the decimal point.
- When rounding, halves are rounded upwards. For example, 2.5 is rounded to 3
- When rounding a number to a given number of decimal places, if the last digit to be lost is 5 or more, the number rounds up. For example, $4.75 = 4.8$ (to 1 decimal place (dp)).
- A number rounded to 1 **significant figure** has only one digit that is not zero. For example, $5735 = 6000$ to one significant figure (1 sf).

Definitions

- **Significant figures** digits, counting from the left, needed to give a number the correct degree of accuracy

Examiner's tips

- When rounding your answer in a GCSE question, be guided by the question. If measurements in the question are to 1 decimal place, give your answer to 1 decimal place.

Can you answer these questions?

1. Work out

   (a) $2.73 + 6.94$ (b) $27.83 - 16.49$ (c) 27.5×4

   (d) 6.94×10 (e) $27.63 \div 100$ (f) $48.4 \div 1000$

   (g) 74.62×1000 (h) 7.29×0.3 (i) 2.15×0.8

2. Work out

   (a) $48.6 \div 2$ (b) $14.4 \div 3$ (c) $183 \div 0.03$

   (d) $17 \div 0.2$ (e) $64 \div 0.04$ (f) $0.63 \div 0.07$

3. Round these numbers to 1 decimal place.

   (a) 6.49 (b) 12.37 (c) 4.51

   (d) 16.85

4. Round these numbers to 1 significant figure.

   (a) 4239 (b) 78 (c) 2055

   (d) 165

5. Romana works for 35 hours in one week. She is paid £7.30 per hour. Work out Romana's pay for the week.

Look on the CD for more exam practice questions

8 Algebra

Key facts

- In **algebra**, letters are used to represent unknown values. An algebraic **expression** must contain at least one letter. $5n - 6$ is an algebraic expression.
- Each part of an expression is called a term of the expression. For example, $5n - 6$ has the terms $5n$ and -6
- There are several rules to follow when writing algebraic expressions.

  $a + a + a = 3a$

  $3 \times a = 3a$ (In algebra the multiplication sign is missed out.)

  $a \times a = a^2$ *not* $2a$

  $a \times a \times a = a^3$ *not* $3a$

  $a \times b \times 2 = 2ab$ The number (called a coefficient) is written first and then the letters are in alphabetical order. There are no multiplication signs.
- Divisions in algebra are usually written as fractions. For example, $\frac{b}{2}$
- $a \times a \times 2 = 2a^2$ *not* $(2a)^2$
- Expressions can be simplified by collecting like terms. Only collect the like terms if the letters and powers are identical.
- To multiply out brackets in an algebraic expression, multiply each term inside the bracket by the term outside the bracket. For example,

  $$3(a+2) = 3a + 6$$

  $$a(a - 4) = a^2 - 4a$$

  This is often called 'expanding brackets'.
- When multiplying out two brackets, each term in the first bracket is multiplied with each term in the second bracket. For example,

  $$\begin{aligned}(n + 4)(n - 1) &= n(n - 1) + 4(n - 1)\\ &= n^2 - n + 4n - 4\\ &= n^2 + 3n - 4\end{aligned}$$
- **Factorising** is the reverse of expanding brackets. An expression is written using brackets by taking out the highest common factor. For example,

  $$6a + 12b = 6(a + 2b)$$

  $$xy + 2y = y(x + 2)$$

  $$2ab + 6bc = 2b(a + 3c)$$
- Two laws of indices that you should know are:

  $$x^n \times x^m = x^{n+m}$$

  $$x^n \div x^m = x^{n-m}$$

▶ continued

- These laws can be used to simplify expressions. For example,

$$x^6 \times x^4 = x^{10}$$
$$x^{12} \div x^2 = x^{10}$$
$$4x^2 \times 3x^5 = 12x^7$$
$$10x^6 \div 2x = 5x^5$$

- When substituting values into expressions, the letters are simply replaced with the given value. For example, if $a = 3$ and $b = -2$, then

$$a^2b = 3^2 \times -2 = 9 \times -2 = -18$$

Definitions

- **algebra** part of mathematics using letters for unknown numbers and variables
- **expression** a statement which can have letters and numbers or both
- **factorising** to break up, or separate, into factors

Examiner's tips

- When asked to factorise expressions remember that you take out the highest common factor.

12a + 24 → 12 $(a + 2)$ → factorised fully

12a + 24 → 6 $(2a + 4)$ → not factorised fully since 6 is not the HCF of 12 and 24

- When expanding brackets like $(n + 2)(n + 3)$ remember to multiply each part. A common error to avoid is adding the two numbers!

Can you answer these questions?

1. A box of crisps contains x packets of plain crisps and y packets of bacon-flavour crisps. Write down an expression, in terms of x and y, for the total number of packets of crisps in the box.
2. Work out the value of each of these expressions when $a = 2$ and $b = 3$

   (a) $2a + b$ (b) $3b - 4$ (c) $5b + a$ (d) $2a^2$ (e) $3b - a^2$
3. Simplify these expressions by collecting like terms.

   (a) $6a - 4a + 3a$ (b) $2b + 6a - a + 4b$ (c) $5c + 2d - 3d - c$
4. Multiply out these brackets.

   (a) $3(n - 1)$ (b) $2(n + 4)$ (c) $a(2a + 1)$ (d) $b(3b - a)$

   (e) $(n + 2)(n + 1)$ (f) $(n - 3)(n - 1)$ (g) $(n - 4)^2$
5. Expand and simplify these.

   (a) $5(2c + d) + 3(c + 2d)$ (b) $5n - 3(n - 1)$
6. Factorise

   (a) $5a + 10$ (b) $16a - 8$ (c) $2y - 3xy$ (d) $8y^2 - 4y$

Look on the CD for more exam practice questions

9 Perimeter and area of 2-D shapes

Key facts

- Perimeter is distance around the edge of 2-D shape.
- Area is amount of space within a 2-D shape.

  area of square = side × side   area of triangle = $\frac{1}{2}$ × base × height

  area of rectangle = length × width   area of parallelogram = base × height

  Measure area in square units. For example, mm^2, cm^2, m^2, km^2
- Converting units

  length: 1 km = 1000 m   1 m = 100 cm   1 cm = 10 mm

  area: 1 km^2 = 1000 m × 1000 m = 1 000 000 m^2

  1 m^2 = 100 cm × 100 cm = 10 000 cm^2

  1 cm^2 = 10 mm × 10 mm = 100 mm^2
- π = circumference ÷ diameter
- circumference of circle = π × diameter = 2 × π × radius
- area of circle = π × radius × radius = πr^2

Definitions

- **Perimeter** the boundary or edge of an enclosed area, as well as the length of that boundary
- **Area** measure, in square units, e.g. mm^2, cm^2, m^2, of the surface of a shape or object

Examiner's tips

- When counting squares to estimate area, add the number of whole squares and those squares that are $\frac{1}{2}$ or more. Ignore squares that are less than half.
- Divide a compound area into 2-D shapes you recognise. Find the area of each part and add them together to find the total area.

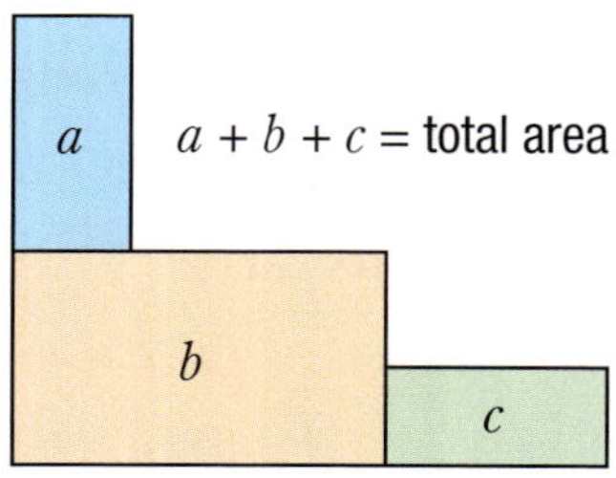

- Count the number of sides of a shape, before calculating perimeter, so you won't forget one.
- Remember to give area in square units, e.g. cm^2

Did you know?

- The word 'perimeter' is Greek for 'around measure'.

Can you answer these questions?

1. Find the area and perimeter of each of these shapes. Use $\pi = 3.142$

(a)

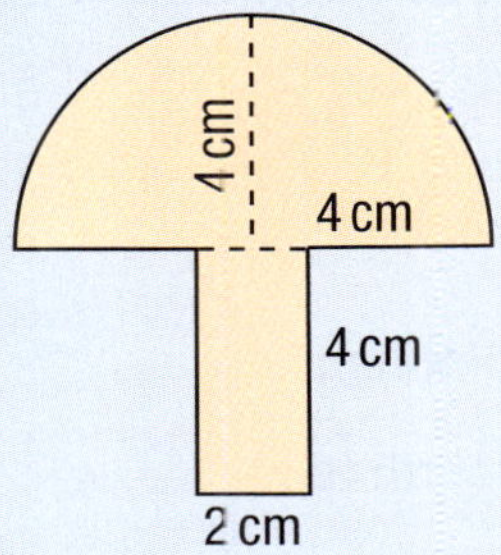

(b)

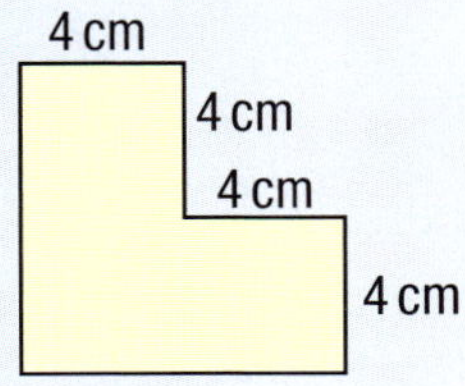

2. Find the shaded area of each of these shapes. Use $\pi = 3.142$

(a)

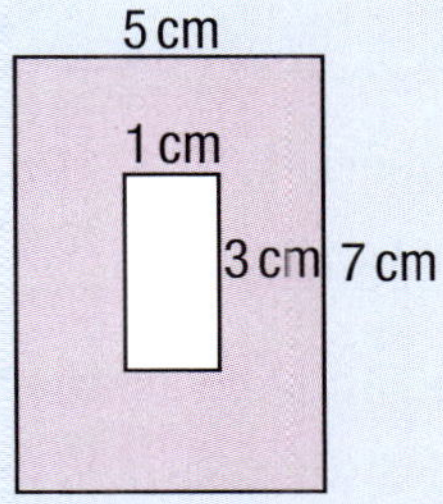

(b)

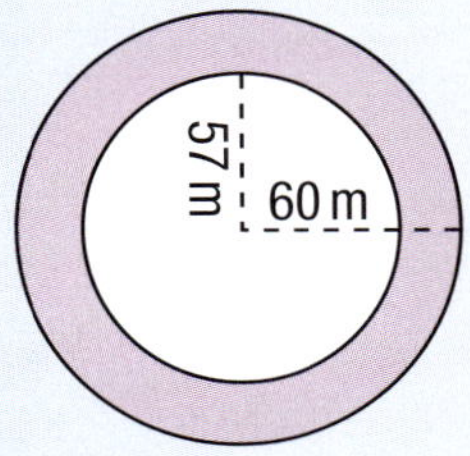

3. Work out the area of these triangles and parallelograms.

(a)

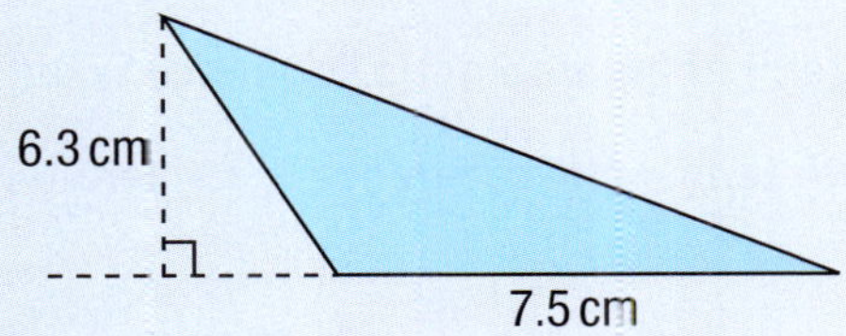

(b)

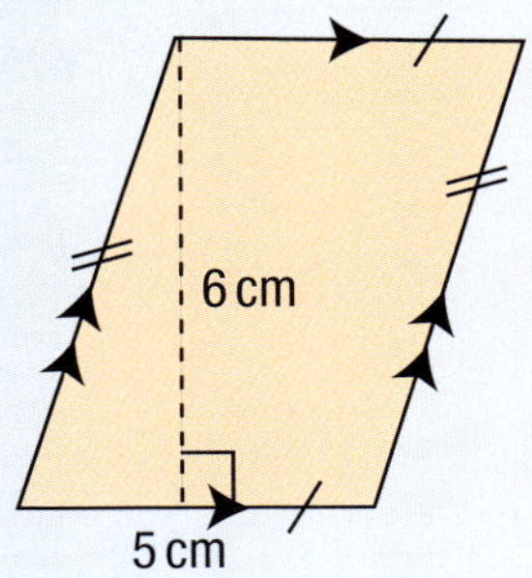

(c)

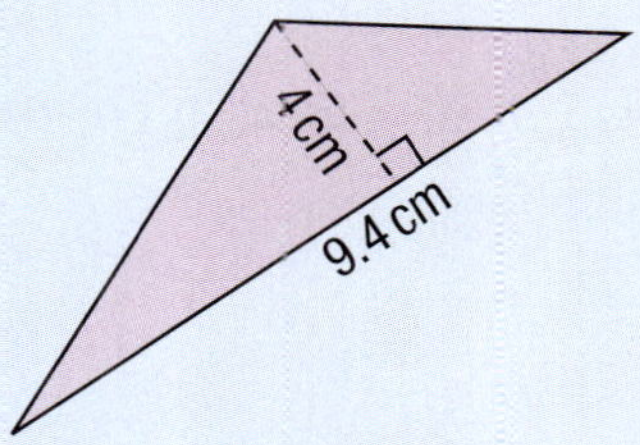

(d)

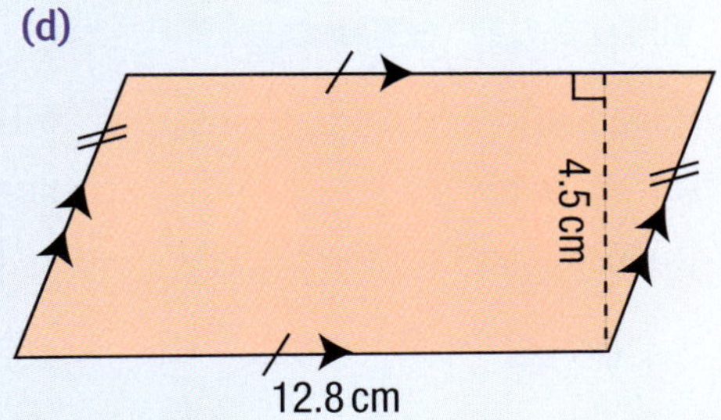

4. Convert the following areas to the units in brackets.

(a) $400\ mm^2$ (cm^2) (b) $64\ km^2$ (m^2)

(c) $25\ m^2$ (mm^2) (d) $1\,000\,000\ cm^2$ (km^2)

Look on the CD for more exam practice questions

10 Sequences

Key facts

- A pattern of shapes or numbers which follow a rule is called a sequence. Each value in a sequence is called a term. For example, in this sequence of numbers, 2, 4, 6, 8, ..., the numbers in the sequence are called terms of the sequence.

  2 is the first term

  8 is the fourth term

- Some common number sequences are:

  square numbers: 1, 4, 9, 16, ...

  cube numbers: 1, 8, 27, 64, ...

  triangular numbers: 1, 3, 6, 10, 15, ...

  the Fibonacci sequence:1, 1, 2, 3, 5, 8, 13, ...

- The function machine can show instructions in a clear way. For example,

$$2a \longrightarrow \boxed{+\,b} \longrightarrow 2a + b$$

- A function is a rule which shows how one set of quantities is related to another. For example, $n \rightarrow 4n - 2$ is a function.
- The nth term of an arithmetic sequence takes the form:

  nth term = the difference $\times\, n$ + zero term

Worked example

Here are the first four terms of an arithmetic sequence: 4, 7, 10, 13, ...

(a) Write down, in terms of n, an expression for this sequence.

(b) Find the 50th term of the sequence.

Solution

(a) The difference between consecutive terms is 3 since $7 - 4 = 3$

The zero term is $4 - 3 = 1$

The nth term is $3n + 1$

(b) nth term is $3n + 1$

50th term is $3 \times 50 + 1 = 150 + 1 = 151$

Definitions

- **Square numbers**
  numbers raised to the power of two; product of 2 equal factors
- **Cube numbers**
  numbers raised to power of three; product of 3 equal factors

Did you know?

- Sequences often appear in nature. The Fibonacci numbers appear in various family trees and patterns of spirals of leaves and seeds.

Look on the CD for more exam practice questions

Examiner's tips

- The rule of a sequence helps you find later terms in a sequence. For example, the rule of the sequence 3, 5, 7, ... is add 2. The nth term of a sequence allows you to find any term in the sequence.

Can you answer these questions?

1. Here is a sequence of numbers:

   60, 54, 48, 42, ...

   (a) Write down the next two numbers in the sequence.

   (b) Write down the rule for this sequence.

2. Here is a sequence of patterns made up of crosses.

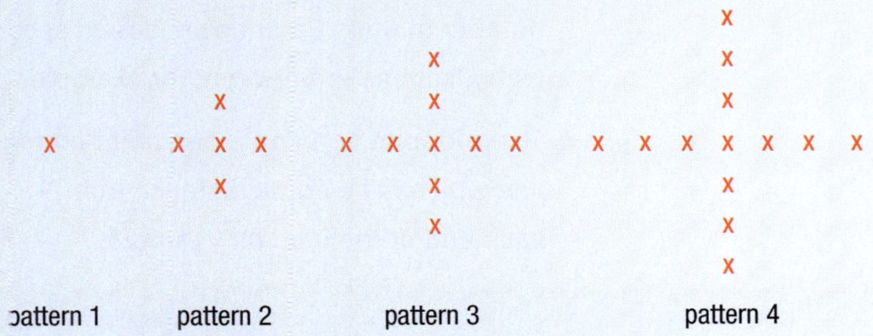

   (a) Write down the rule for this sequence.

   (b) Draw pattern 5

   (c) Complete the table.

Pattern number	1	2	3	4	5	6
Number of crosses	1	5	9			

3. Write down, in terms of n, an expression for the nth term of these sequences.

   (a) 2, 4, 6, 8, ...   (b) 4, 9, 14, 19, ...   (c) 5, 8, 11, 14, ...

11 Graphs

Key facts

- Coordinates are used to describe the position of a point.

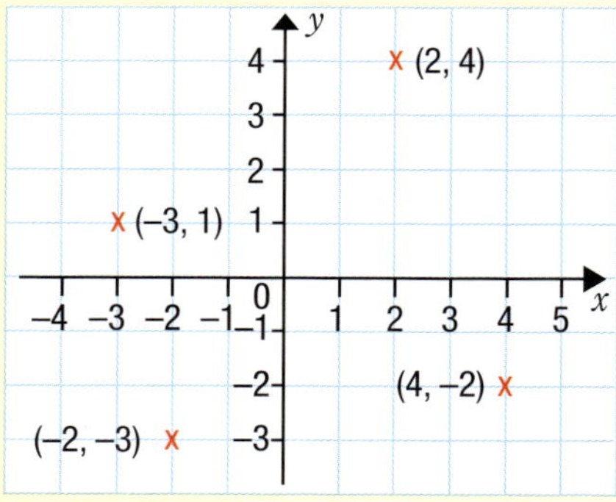

- When reading coordinates the number of units across is read first, and the number of units up or down is read second. They are always put in brackets with a comma in between, for example, (2, 3).
- The midpoint of a line is the point on the line which is an equal distance from each end of the line, for example,

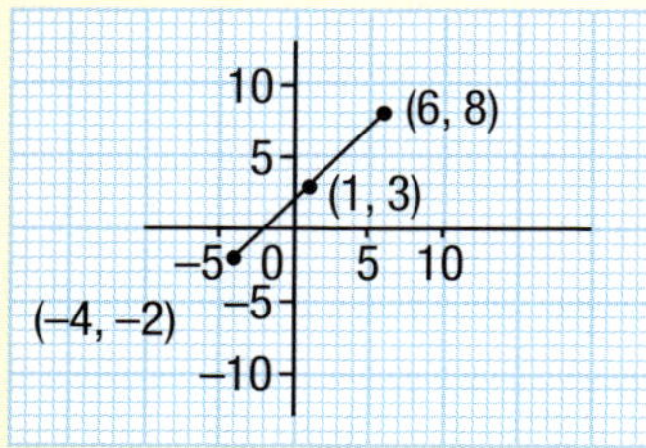

  The coordinates of the midpoint are (1, 3).
- Straight line (linear) graphs are often used to show the relationships between different amounts, for example, conversion graphs.
- Conversion graphs are used to convert one measurement into another measurement, for example, litres to pints, km to miles, etc

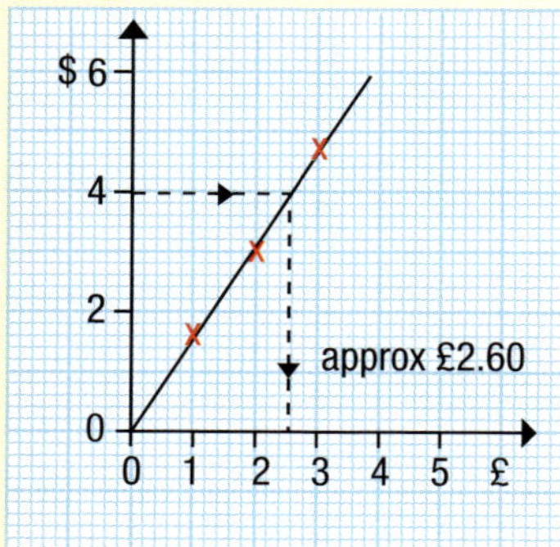

- You can solve problems involving distance and time by drawing distance–time graphs. These are sometimes called 'travel graphs'.

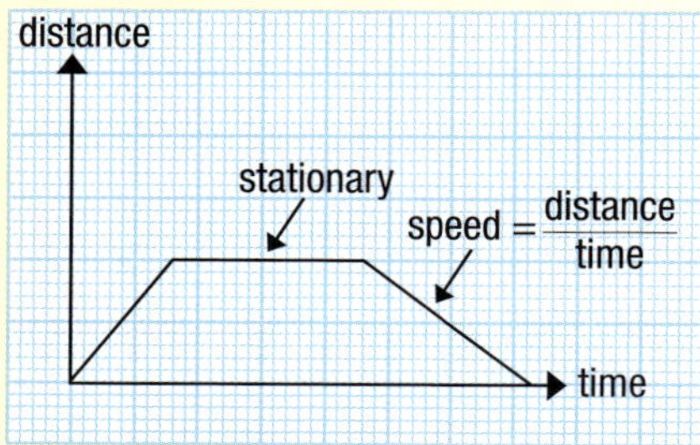

▶ continued

- The line $y = b$ is a horizontal line where every y-coordinate is equal to b.

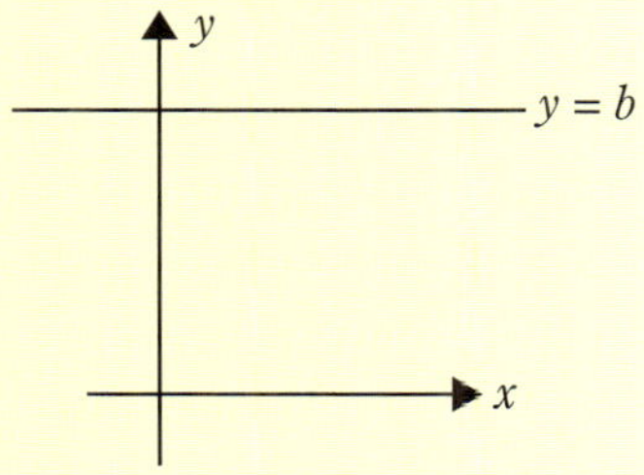

- The line $x = a$ is a vertical line where every x-coordinate is equal to a.

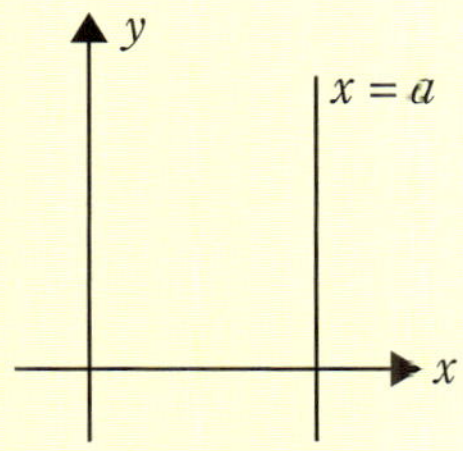

- Graphs of the form $y = mx + c$ are straight line graphs.

  m represents the gradient of the line.

  c represents the intercept on the y-axis.

  The greater the value of m, the steeper the line.

- The gradient of a straight line is found by:

  $$\text{gradient} = \frac{\text{vertical distance}}{\text{horizontal distance}}$$

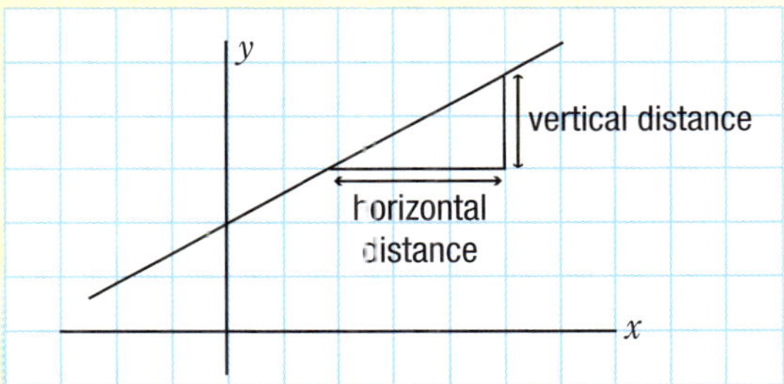

- Graphs of the functions of the form $y = x^2 + a$, where a can be positive, negative or zero, are all ∪– shaped. These are called quadratic graphs. The bottom of the curve cuts the y-axis at (0, a). Quadratic graphs are often known as parabolas.

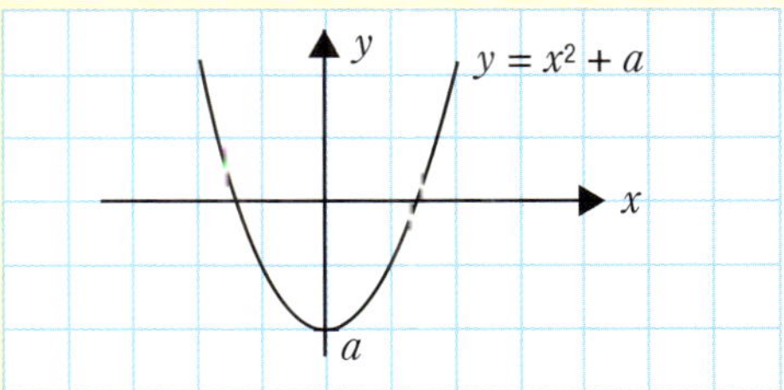

- Quadratic graphs of the form $y = -ax^2$ are ∩– shaped.
- Graphs of quadratic functions can be used to solve quadratic equations.

Worked example

The grid shows the graph of $y = x^2$.

Use the graph to find an estimate to the solution $x^2 = 7$

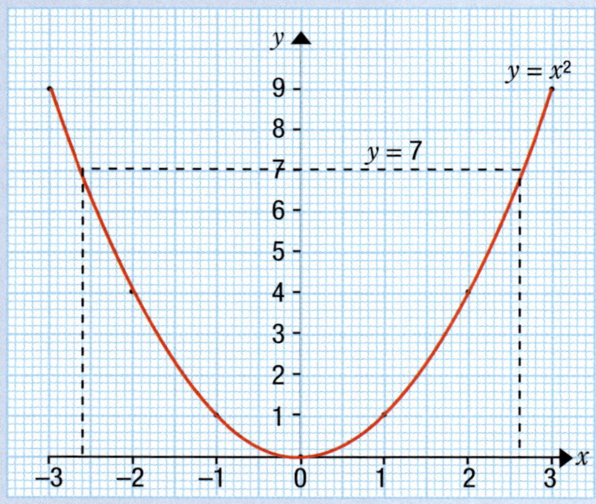

Solution

Draw a line across from $y = 7$

Read off the coordinates where the line $y = 7$ meets the graph $y = x^2$.

The solutions are $x = 2.6$ and -2.6

Examiner's tips

- When drawing quadratic graphs use a pencil and join the points with as smooth a curve as possible.

Look on the CD for more exam practice questions

Can you answer these questions?

1. (a) Write down the coordinates of the points A to E.

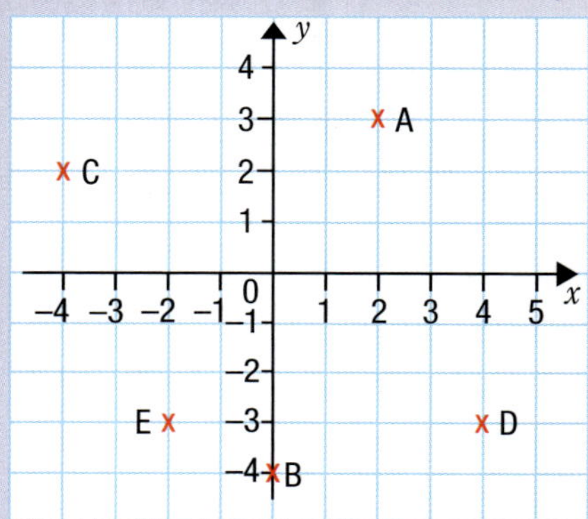

   (b) Write down the coordinates of the midpoint of a line which joins A to D.

2. (a) Draw the graph of $y = 5x - 2$ Use values of x from -2 to 3

   (b) The point with the coordinate $(k, 7)$ lies on the graph of $y = 5x - 2$ Use your graph to find the value of k.

3. For each of these lines write down the (i) gradient (ii) y-intercept

   (a) $y = 5x + 1$ (b) $y = 2 - 4x$

2 Fractions 2

Key facts

- To find a fraction of a quantity, multiply the fraction by the quantity. For example,

  $$\frac{2}{3} \text{ of } 24 = \frac{2}{3} \times 24 = \frac{48}{3} = 16$$

- To express one amount as a fraction of another amount, write them as a fraction with the first amount as the numerator and the second amount as the denominator. (Both amounts must be in the same units.)
- To add and subtract fractions, the fractions must be written with the same denominator. For example,

  $$\frac{1}{3} + \frac{5}{6} = \frac{2}{6} + \frac{5}{6} = \frac{7}{6} = 1\frac{1}{6}$$

- To multiply fractions, write out whole or **mixed numbers** as **improper fractions** before starting. Then multiply the two numerators together and then the two denominators. For example,

  $$\frac{3}{7} \times \frac{4}{9} = \frac{12}{63} \quad \text{Simplify this answer to } \frac{4}{21}$$

- To divide fractions, write out whole or mixed numbers as improper fractions before starting. Then turn the second fraction upside down and multiply it with the first. For example,

  $$3\frac{1}{2} \div \frac{4}{5}$$

  $$= \frac{7}{2} \div \frac{4}{5}$$

  $$= \frac{7}{2} \times \frac{5}{4}$$

  $$= \frac{35}{8}$$

  $$= 4\frac{3}{8}$$

Definitions

- **Improper fraction** fraction with numerator greater than its demoninator
- **Mixed number** includes both a whole number and fractional part

Examiner's tips

- When finding a fraction of a quantity, divide the quantity by the denominator first to work out one part of the amount and then multiply by the numerator.

Can you answer these questions?

1. Find $\frac{2}{3}$ of (a) 9 (b) 27
2. There are 850 students in a school. $\frac{2}{5}$ of the students come to school by coach. Work out the number of students in the school who come to school by coach.
3. Express the first amount as a fraction of the second amount. Give your fraction in its simplest form.
   (a) £35 and £60 (b) 18 kg and 24 kg
4. Work out
   (a) $\frac{2}{3} + \frac{1}{2}$ (b) $\frac{5}{7} - \frac{1}{3}$ (c) $2\frac{4}{5} + 3\frac{2}{7}$
5. Work out
   (a) $5 \times \frac{1}{6}$ (b) $\frac{1}{4} \times \frac{2}{7}$ (c) $\frac{9}{10} \times \frac{6}{13}$
6. Work out
   (a) $\frac{2}{5} \div \frac{4}{9}$ (b) $\frac{12}{15} \div \frac{11}{30}$ (c) $3\frac{1}{4} \div 1\frac{2}{5}$

Look on the CD for more exam practice questions

13 Processing, representing and interpreting data

Key facts

- Discrete data has separate values, e.g. shoe size.
- Continuous data has continuous values, e.g. height.
- A pictogram has pictures or symbols to represent discrete data.

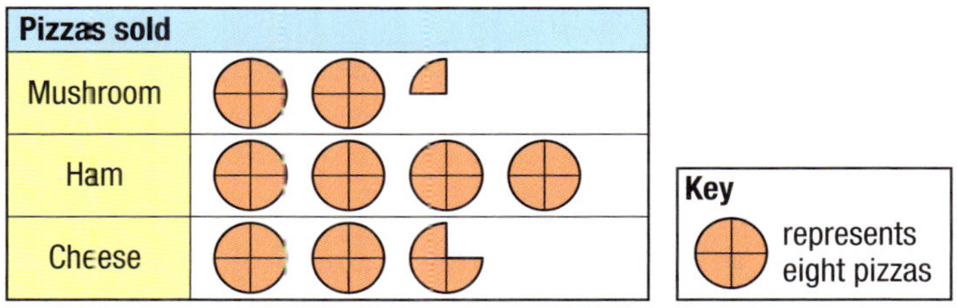

- A bar chart has bars of equal width to represent frequency of discrete data.

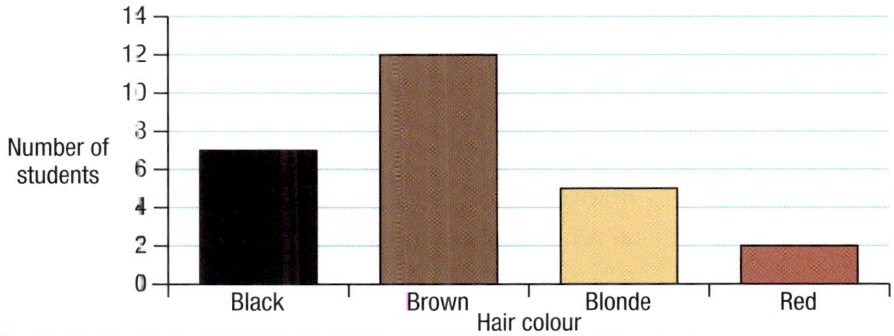

- A pie chart is a circle divided into slices that represent frequency of discrete data. The slice size is given by the angle at the centre of the slice. (To find slice angle, use 360° ÷ total frequency for 1 item of data and multiply this by number of items in each section.)

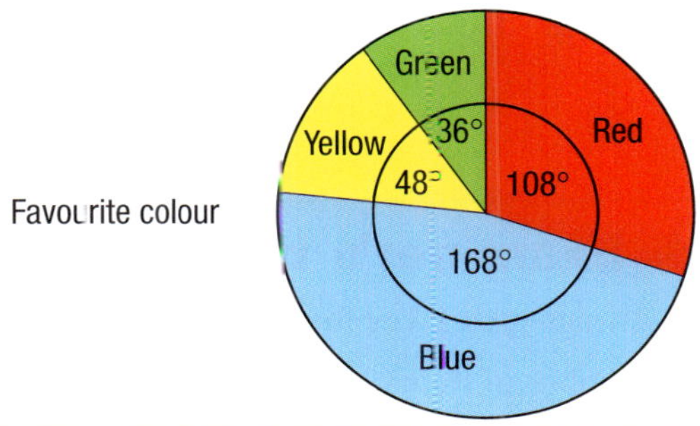

- A time series is a set of readings taken over a period of time and is used to draw a line graph.

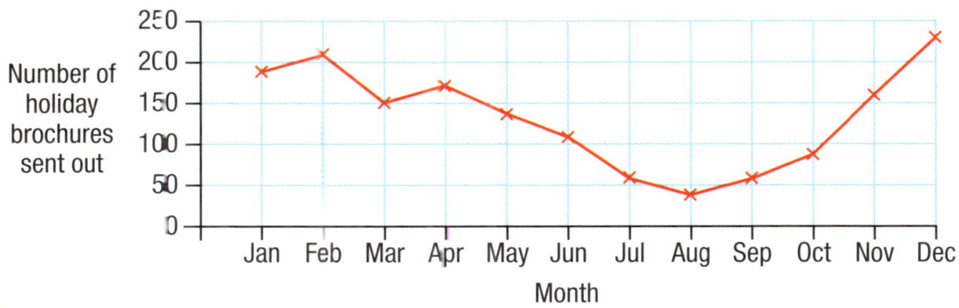

* A frequency diagram represents grouped discrete data.

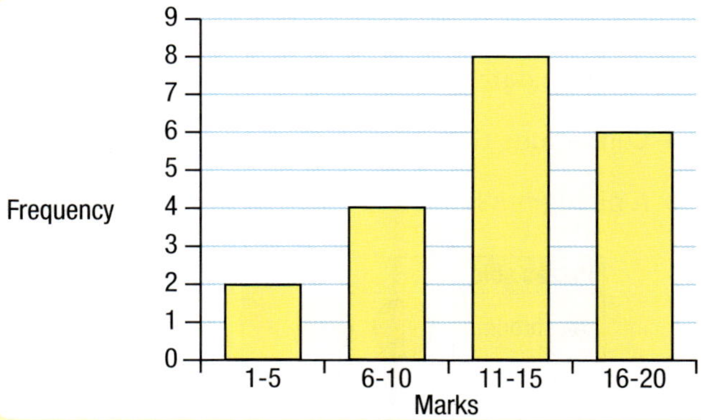

* A frequency polygon compares 2 or more sets of data.

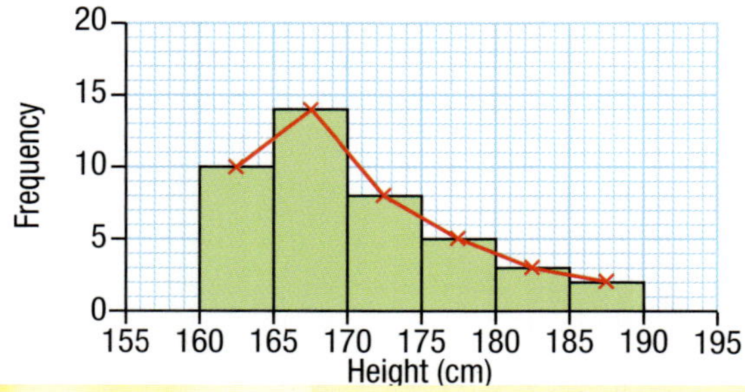

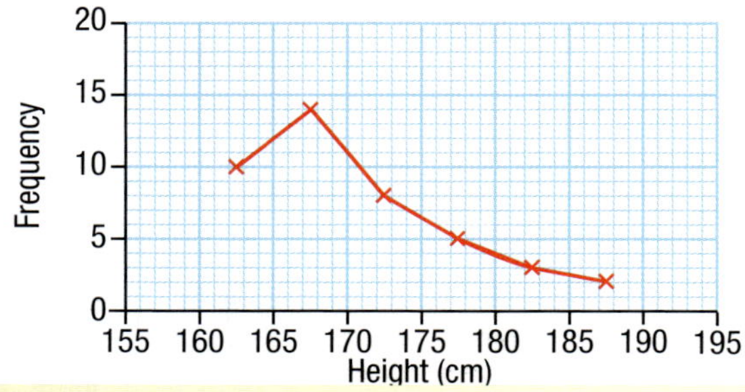

* A histogram has bars that represent continuous data.

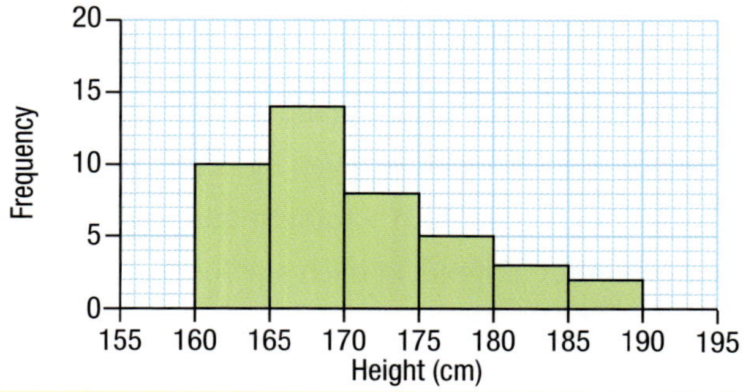

Examiner's tips

* Always give a key for a pictogram, showing symbol used to represent a number of items.
* The sum of the angles for each sector of a pie chart should total 360°.
* Marks are given for correct labels and angles on a pie chart.
* Marks are given for pie chart angle calculations, e.g. 360° ÷ total number of items.
* A bar chart has gaps between the bars and labels on the horizontal axis.
* A histogram has no gaps between the bars and a scale on the horizontal axis.
* A frequency polygon is drawn by joining midpoints of class intervals with straight lines.

Did you know?

- In 1858, Florence Nightingale began using her own version of pie charts to present data.

Can you answer these questions?

1. Draw a pictogram to illustrate the sports played by students in Year 10

Sport	Number of students
Football	20
Cricket	14
Tennis	10
Swimming	15
Squash	6
Hockey	15

2. Draw a pie chart from this table.

Favourite pet	Number of students
Dog	9
Cat	8
Fish	10
Rabbit	5
Rat	4

3

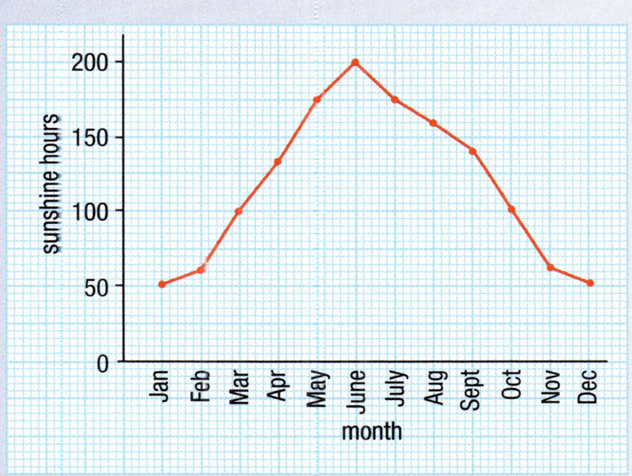

Use this line graph, showing average hours of sunshine per month in Birmingham, to answer these questions.

(a) Which was the sunniest month?

(b) How many hours of sunshine were there in March?

(c) What was the year total of hours of sunshine?

4. Draw a frequency polygon to show distance travelled in km by Year 11 students using the midpoints of the intervals in this table.

Distance (d) travelled by Year 11 pupils (km)	Number of students
$0 \leqslant d < 1$	10
$1 \leqslant d < 2$	12
$2 \leqslant d < 3$	18
$3 \leqslant d < 4$	8
$4 \leqslant d < 5$	7
$5 \leqslant d < 6$	5

Look on the CD for more exam practice questions

14 Measure

Have you ever wondered?

Why are there 60 seconds in a minute, 60 minutes in an hour and 366 days in a leap year?

Key facts

- You can tell the time on:

  analogue clock: hands on clock face give only 12-hour time (am for times before midday, pm for times after midday)

  digital clock: shows numbers and can give either 12-hour or 24-hour time.

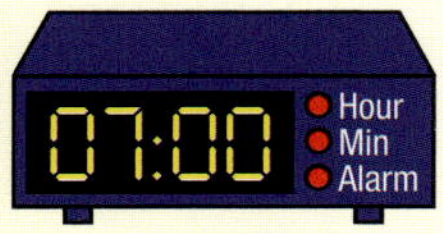

- To convert between 12-hour time and 24-hour time:

  include 0 to make 4 digits, e.g. 8.30am → 0830

  add 12 to the hour if pm, e.g. 4.15pm → 1615

- Units

  length: 1 km = 1000 m   1 m = 100 cm   1 cm = 10 mm

  weight: 1 tonne = 1000 kg   1 kg = 1000 g   1 g = 1000 mg

  capacity/volume: 1 litre = 1000 cm^3 = 1000 ml = 100 cl

- Compound measures

  speed = distance ÷ time

  density = mass ÷volume

Examiner's tips

- When calculating time, remember that 60 seconds = 1 minute
  60 minutes = 1 hour.
  For example, 1 hour 23 minutes + 3 hours 45 minutes = 5 hours 8 minutes
- Give time correctly. For example, 5.10pm or 1710   510 is not acceptable.
- Remember speed calculations using

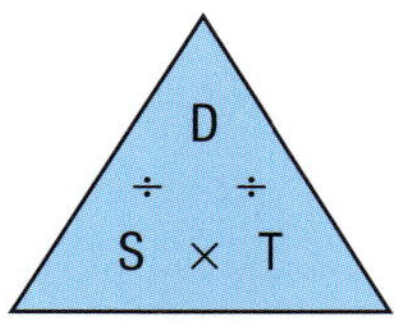

- Remember average speed = total distance travelled ÷ total time taken
- Remember density calculations using

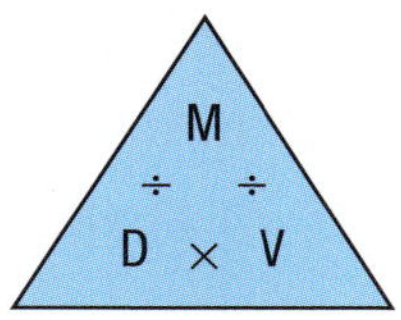

Definitions

- **Speed** distance travelled per unit time
- **Density** mass per unit volume of an object

Did you know?

- Some imperial units of measurement were based on parts of the body. For example, 1foot was the average length of a man's foot.

Look on the CD for more exam practice questions

Can you answer these questions?

1. Write down the reading from each of these scales.

(a)

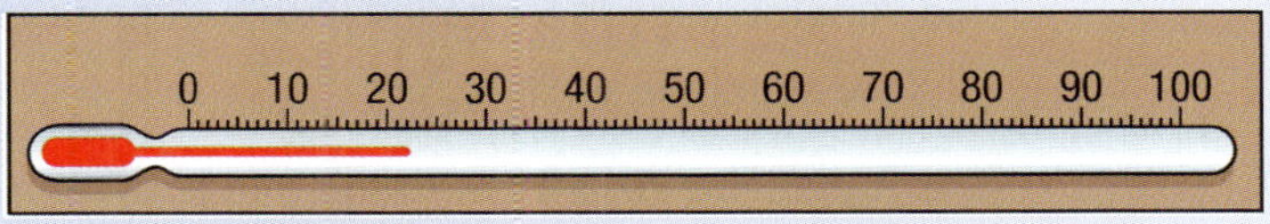

(b)

(c)

(d)

2. Convert these times to 24-hour clock.

(a) 11.35am (b) 12.05am (c) 7.56pm

3. Convert these times to 12-hour clock.

(a) 2110 (b) 0235 (c) 1215

4. This is a timetable of some trains travelling to London Victoria.

Eastbourne	dep	1131	—	1145	—	1158	1202	—	1231	—
Hampden Park	dep	—	—	—	—	1202	1206	—	—	—
Polegate	dep	1137	—	1152	—	1206	1211	—	1237	—
Berwick	dep	—	—	—	—	—	1217	—	—	—
Glynde	dep	—	—	—	—	—	1222	—	—	—
Seaford	dep	—	—	—	1158	—	—	1225	—	—
Bishopstone	dep	—	—	—	1200	—	—	1227	—	—
Newhaven Harbour	dep	—	—	—	1203	—	—	1230	—	—
Newhaven Town	dep	—	—	—	1205	—	—	1232	—	—
Southease	dep	—	—	—	—	—	—	1236	—	—
Lewes	arr	1149	—	1207	1214	1218	1228	1244	1249	—
Lewes	dep	1150	1158	1207	1214	1220	1228	1244	1250	1258
Falmer	dep	—	1205	—	1221	—	1235	1251	—	1305
Moulsecomb	dep	—	1208	—	1224	—	1238	1254	—	1308
London Road (Brighton)	dep	—	1210	—	1227	—	1240	1257	—	1310
Brighton	arr	—	1214	1220	1230	—	1244	1300	—	1314
Cooksbridge	dep	—	—	—	—	—	—	—	—	—
Plumpton	dep	—	—	—	—	1228	—	—	—	—
Wivelsfield	arr	—	—	—	—	1234	—	—	—	—
Haywards Heath	arr	1205	—	—	—	1240	—	—	1310	—
Haywards Heath	dep	1215	—	—	—	1243	—	—	1313	—
Three Bridges	arr	—	—	—	—	—	—	—	—	—
Gatwick Airport	arr	1224	—	—	—	1254	—	—	1324	—
East Croydon	arr	1240	—	—	—	1310	—	—	1340	—
East Croydon	dep	1247	—	—	—	1317	—	—	1347	—
London Bridge	arr	1300b	—	—	—	1330b	—	—	1400b	—
East Croydon	dep	1240	—	—	—	1310	—	—	1340	—
Clapham Junction	arr	1249	—	—	—	1319	—	—	1349	—
London Victoria	arr	1257	—	—	—	1327	—	—	1357	—

(a) How long does it take to travel from Haywards Heath to Victoria if leaving at 1313?

(b) Which is the fastest train from Eastbourne to Haywards Heath?

(c) Which is the (i) last morning train from Seaford to Victoria (ii) first afternoon train from Lewes to Victoria?

5. Convert these measurements to the units given in brackets.

(a) 155 mm (cm) (b) 2.6 km (m) (c) 1500 m (cm) (d) 300 000 cm (km)

6. (a) How long does it take to travel 200 miles at 70mph?

(b) How far can you travel in $2\frac{1}{2}$ hours at 4km/h?

(c) What is the density of 1 litre of a substance with mass of 980 g?

15 Percentages

Key facts

- A percentage is a fraction with a denominator of 100
  For example, $63\% = \frac{63}{100}$
- A percentage can be changed to a fraction in its simplest form.
  For example, $40\% = \frac{40}{100} = \frac{2}{5}$ in its simplest form.
- A percentage can be changed into a decimal.
  For example $32\% = \frac{32}{100} = 0.32$
- 'Of' means multiply.
- To find a percentage of a quantity, change the percentage to a fraction or a decimal and multiply it by the quantity.
  For example, 24% of £70 $= \frac{24}{100} \times$ £70 = £16.80
- To write a quantity as a percentage of another quantity:
  Write down the first quantity as a fraction of the second quantity.
  Change the fraction to a percentage by multiplying by 100
- When asked to write a list of fractions, decimals and percentages in order of size, change all the numbers to decimals so that they can be compared.
- To increase or decrease a quantity by a percentage, work out the percentage of a quantity first and then increase or decrease the original by that amount.

Worked examples

Example 1

Write 24 as a percentage of 30

Solution 1

$\frac{24}{30} \times 100\% = 80\%$

Example 2

A plasma TV costs £1999. In a sale it is reduced by 30%. Work out the sale price of the TV.

Solution 2

Method 1

30% of £1999

$= \frac{30}{100} \times$ £1999

= £599.70

Sale price

= £1999 − £599.70

= £1399.30

Method 2

100% − 30% = 70%

70% = 0.7

0.7 × £1999 = £1399.30

Sale price = £1399.30

▶ continued

Example 3

A car **depreciates** by 10% each year. If the car was £12 000 when new, what would it be worth after 2 years?

Solution 3

Work out 10% of £12 000 $\frac{10}{100} \times 12\,000 = £1200$

£12 000 − £1200 = £10 800 (price after year 1)

Work out 10% of £10 800, the value of the car after year 1

$\frac{10}{100} \times £10\,800 = £1080$

After 2 years the car is worth £10 800 − £1080 = £9720

Definitions

- **Depreciate**
  decrease in value

Examiner's tips

- If you have a question which asks you to work out a repeated price increase or decrease, then remember to work it out year on year.

Can you answer these questions?

1. Write each percentage as
   (i) a fraction (ii) a decimal.
   (a) 62% (b) 45% (c) 79%
2. Write these numbers in order of size. Start with the smallest.
   48% 0.4 $\frac{9}{20}$ $\frac{5}{8}$
3. Work out
   (a) 37% of 60 kg
   (b) 85% of £2700
4. The price of a computer is £650
   In a sale it is reduced by 15%. Work out the sale price of the computer.
5. Samuel invests £650
   The interest rate is 4% per year. How much will Samuel have in his bank account at the end of one year?
6. Write 27 kg out of 120 kg as a percentage.
7. Emily scored 17 out of 30 in a test. Work out her score as a percentage.

Look on the CD for more exam practice questions

16 Averages and ranges

Have you ever wondered?

Why do we have 3 different averages?

Key facts

- There are 3 **averages** used in statistics:

  mean = total frequency ÷ number of items

  median = middle number, when numbers are placed in order

  mode = most frequent number.

- Averages can be found using:

  frequency tables

  stem and leaf diagrams (data arranged in the form of a stem (tens)) and leaf (units).

0	6	6	8					
1	2	2	4	7				
2	0	0	1	1	3	3	3	6
3	0	4	5	5	9			
4	1	3						

- Back-to-back stem and leaf diagrams can be used to compare 2 sets of data, e.g. using mode and **range**.

  (See question 3.)

Definitions

- **Average** normal or standard amount of value
- **Range** difference between greatest and least values of data

Examiner's tips

- Arrange data in ascending order in order to find the middle value or median.
- Use middle value of class interval to calculate estimated mean.
- A key is useful in a stem and leaf diagram, e.g. 1|5 means 15

Can you answer these questions?

1. The height of a sample group of 10 students, from 3 different school years, is measured.

   Calculate the mean, median and mode and range for these.

   (a) 134 cm 135 cm 127 cm 133 cm 141 cm 133 cm 127 cm 133 cm 133 cm 134 cm

   (b) 159 cm 156 cm 159 cm 152 cm 149 cm 156 cm 156 cm 156 cm 153 cm 158 cm

   (c) Draw a stem and leaf diagram and use it to find the median and range for these.

   176 cm 176 cm 177 cm 165 cm 174 cm 174 cm 186 cm 174 cm 174 cm 168 cm

2. Year 10 students choose these sports for their games period.

   Calculate the mean number of students for each sport, and the median and mode sport from this table.

Sport	Number of students
Cricket	12
Rounders	12
Swimming	10
Athletics	13
Badminton	5
Tennis	8

3. 2 groups of plants are measured, in centimetres, after 10 days. Use this back-to-back stem and leaf diagram to comment on their progress.

X		Y
0	0	7
6 5 3 2	1	3 4 4 7 8
6 6 6 5 2 1 0	2	1 1 1 4 4 5 7
9 9 8 8 1 1	3	2 3 3 4 4 5
3 2 1 1 0	4	0 6 7 9

4. Calculate the (a) modal class (b) range of weights (c) estimated mean weight of apples in this grouped data table.

Weight (w) of apples (g)	Frequency
$100 \leqslant w < 110$	4
$110 \leqslant w < 120$	8
$120 \leqslant w < 130$	15
$130 \leqslant w < 140$	10
$140 \leqslant w < 150$	7
$150 \leqslant w < 160$	6

Look on the CD for more exam practice questions

17 Equations and inequalities

Key facts

- When asked to solve an equation, you are being asked to find the value of the unknown letter that makes the equation true.
- The balance method is used to solve linear equations, i.e. whatever is done to one side of the equation must be done to the other.
- Cubic equations can be solved by trial and improvement.
- The signs used for inequalities are:

$<$	less than	$>$	greater than
$\leqslant$	less than or equal to	$\geqslant$	greater than or equal to

- Inequalities can be shown on a number line. For example,

  The inequality $-2 < x \leqslant 3$ is shown as

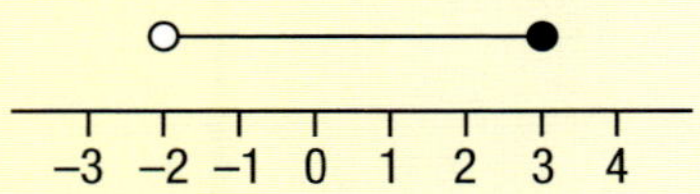

  The open circle (○) indicates that the –2 is not included.

  The closed circle (●) indicates that the 3 is included.

- When finding **integer** solutions to inequalities a number line can be used. For example, the integer solutions to the inequality $-3 < n \leqslant 1$ are
  –2 –1 0 1

Worked examples

Example 1

Solve the equation $5x - 2 = 8$

Solution 1

$5x - 2 = 8$

$5x - 2 + 2 = 8 + 2$ Add 2 to both sides.

$5x = 10$

$x = 10 \div 5$ Divide both sides by 5

$x = 2$

Example 2

Solve the equation $3(a + 2) = 15$

Solution 2

$3(a + 2) = 15$

$3a + 6 = 15$ Multiply out the brackets.

$3a + 6 - 6 = 15 - 6$ Subtract 6 from both sides.

$3a = 9$

$a = 9 \div 3$

$a = 3$

Example 3

Solve the equation $4(3y - 1) = 8y - 8$

Solution 3

$4(3y - 1) = 8y - 8$

$12y - 4 = 8y - 8$

$12y - 4 - 8y = -8$ Subtract $8y$ from both sides.

$4y - 4 = -8$

$4y = -4$ Add 4 to both sides.

$y = -1$ Divide both sides by 4

Definitions

- **Integer** any whole number, positive or negative, including zero

Examiner's tips

- When solving equations it is really important to show your working out, even though it might be tempting to work it out mentally. Showing working out helps you get the right answer and score valuable method marks.

Can you answer these questions?

1. Solve these equations
   (a) $n - 6 = 10$ (b) $2n = 12$ (c) $\frac{n}{3} = 6$
   (d) $5n - 3 = 12$ (e) $6 - 2n = 10$ (f) $5 + 2n = 4$
2. Solve these equations
   (a) $2(n - 1) = 12$ (b) $3(2n + 1) = 15$ (c) $4(3n - 2) = 16$
3. Solve these equations
   (a) $4x = 2x + 3$ (b) $5x - 1 = 3x + 5$ (c) $3x - 1 = x + 6$
   (d) $3(2x - 1) = 4x + 5$ (e) $\frac{x}{4} = x - 1$ (f) $\frac{x}{3} = 2x - 3$
4. The diagram shows a triangle. The perimeter of the triangle is 30 cm.
   Work out the value of x.

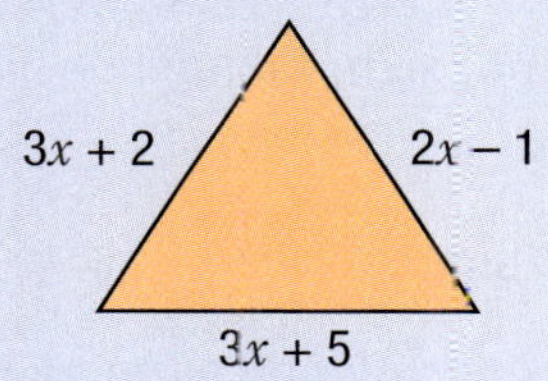

5 (a) On a number line, show the inequality $-2 \leqslant p < 5$
   (b) Write down all the integer values of p.
6. Solve these inequalities
   (a) $n + 2 < 6$ (b) $4n - 1 < 11$ (c) $6x \leqslant 2x + 4$

Look on the CD for more exam practice questions

18 Powers and roots

Key facts

- An **index** can also be called a power. Repeated multiplication by the same number can be written in the form:

  the index or power

  a^b

  the base

  For example, $4^7 = 4 \times 4 \times 4 \times 4 \times 4 \times 4 \times 4$

- Square numbers are obtained by multiplying a whole number by itself. For example,

  $5^2 = 5 \times 5 = 25$

- Cube numbers are obtained by multiplying a whole number by itself and then multiplying by the number again. For example, $6^3 = 6 \times 6 \times 6 = 216$

- $\sqrt{}$ is the square root sign. Finding the square root is the opposite of squaring. For example,

  $\sqrt{64} = 8$ or -8 since $8^2 = 64$ and $-8^2 = 64$

- $\sqrt[3]{}$ is the cube root sign. Taking the cube root is the opposite of cubing. For example,

  $\sqrt[3]{27} = 3$ since $3^3 = 27$

- There are a few rules of indices you need to know:

  when multiplying, add the indices $x^n \times x^m = x^{n+m}$

  when dividing, subtract the indices $x^n \div x^m = x^{n-m}$

- BIDMAS is an acronym which helps you remember the order in which calculations take place.

  Brackets

  Indices (powers)

  Division

  Multiplication

  Addition

  Subtraction

  For example, $8^2 + (2 \times 6) = 76$ not 396 since 2×6 is calculated first.

- The reciprocal of a number is what it has to be multiplied by to get 1 as the answer. For example, the reciprocal of 5 is $\frac{1}{5}$

Definitions

- **Index** small digit to the right of a number, or letter, giving the number of times it is multiplied by itself

Did you know?

- Basic calculators do not follow BIDMAS so check your calculation mentally.

Look on the CD for more exam practice questions

Examiner's tips

- Remember that the square root of a number has two possible values, the positive square root and the negative square root. For example, $\sqrt{100} = 10$ and -10

Can you answer these questions?

1. Write as powers
   (a) $4 \times 4 \times 4 \times 4 \times 4$
   (b) $3 \times 3 \times 3 \times 3 \times 3 \times 3$
2. Work out
   (a) 5^3 (b) 6^4
   (c) 2^6 (d) $2^3 + 3^2$
3. Work out
   (a) $\sqrt{81}$ (b) $\sqrt[3]{125}$
   (c) $\sqrt[3]{81}$ (d) $\sqrt{144}$
4. Work out
   (a) 3×2^3 (b) $4 + 3^2$
   (c) $4^2 + (2 \times 3)$
5. Write as powers of 5
   (a) $5^6 \times 5^3$ (b) $5^7 \div 5^4$
   (c) $\dfrac{5 \times 5^3}{5^2}$ (d) $\dfrac{5^9 \times 5^4}{5^6}$

19 Formulae

Key facts

- A formula is a way of describing a fact or a rule. A formula can be written in words or using algebraic **expressions**.

  For example, area of a rectangle = length × width (word formula)

  $A = l \times w$ (algebraic formula)

- In the formula $A = l \times w$, the A appears on its own on the left-hand side of the formula. This is called the 'subject of the formula'.
- Substitution into a formula is when the letters in the formula are replaced with the given value.

  For example, $a = \frac{bc}{2}$ if $b = 12$ and $c = 4$ find a

  $a = \frac{12 \times 4}{2}$

  $a = 24$

- The subject of a formula can be changed by using the balance method.

Worked example

Make b the subject of the formula $a = 3b + c$

Solution

$a = 3b + c$

$a - c = 3b + c - c$ Subtract c from both sides.

$\frac{a - c}{3} = \frac{3b}{3}$ Divide both sides by 3.

$\frac{a - c}{3} = b$ b is now the subject.

Definitions

- **Expression** statement with letters or numbers or both

Examiner's tips

- When changing the subject of a formula, take care that you work through it step by step.

Look on the CD for more exam practice questions

Can you answer these questions?

1. Use the formula pay = rate of pay × hours worked to work out the pay that Charlotte receives if she works 30 hours at a rate of pay of £7.20 per hour.
2. The sweets in a packet are shared equally between 5 people. Write down a word formula that can be used to work out the number of sweets that each person receives.
3. The formula $v = u + at$ is used to work out the final velocity, v. Use the formula to work out the value of v when $u = 6$ $a = 10$ $t = 3$
4. A stationery shop sells x pencils at 20p each and y pens at 90p each. If C is the total cost in pence of the stationery sold, write down in terms of x and y a formula for C.
5. $a = bc + d$ Make c the subject of the formula.
6. $p = a^2b + 2c$ Make c the subject of the formula.

20 Circumference and area of a circle

Key facts

- The circumference (or **perimeter**) of a circle is the distance around the outside edge.

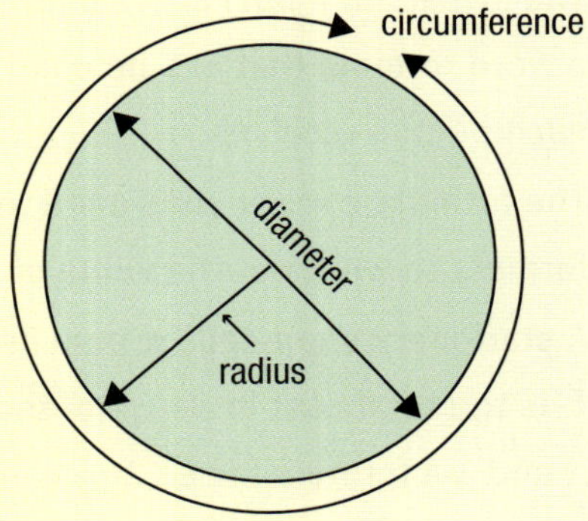

- The circumference of a circle can be found by using the formulae:

  Circumference of a circle = $\pi \times$ diameter

  $C = \pi \times d$

  or

  Circumference of a circle = $2 \times \pi \times$ radius

  $C = 2 \times \pi \times r$

- To find the diameter of a circle, divide its circumference by π, $d = \frac{C}{\pi}$
- The area of a circle can be found by using this formula:

  Area of circle = $\pi \times (\text{radius})^2$

  $A = \pi \times r^2$

- Answers to questions involving circumference and area of a circle can be expressed in terms of π.

Definitions

- **Perimeter** the boundary or edge of an enclosed area, as well as the length of that boundary

Examiner's tips

- You need to learn the formulae for circumference and area of a circle and try not to confuse $2r$ with r^2. Remember r^2 means $r \times r$.
- If you do not have a calculator leave your answer in terms of π.

Can you answer these questions?

1. Work out the circumference of these circles. Use $\pi = 3.142$

(a)

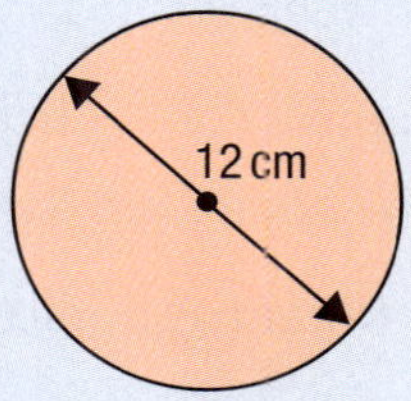

(b)

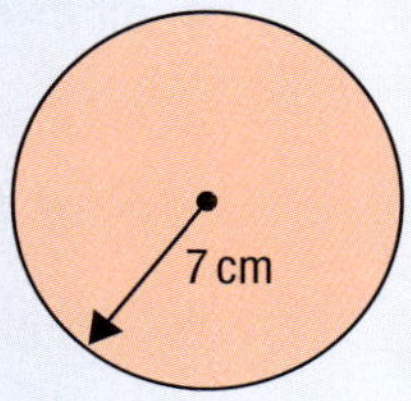

(c)

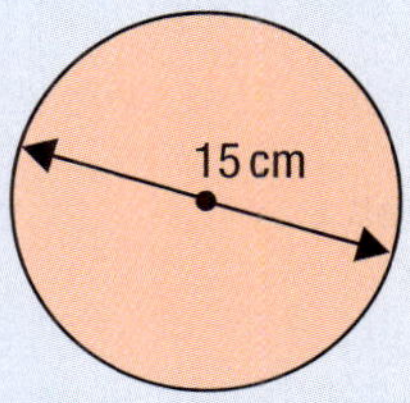

(d)

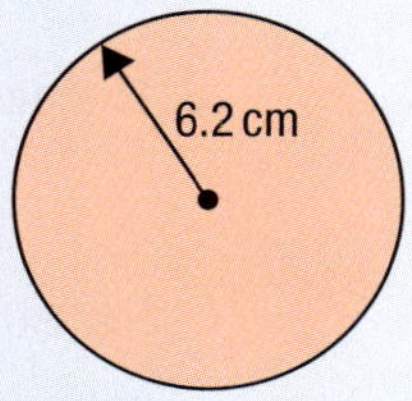

2. The circumference of a circle is 24.6 cm. Work out its radius. Give your answer correct to 2 decimal places.

3. A semicircle has a diameter of 20 cm. Work out its perimeter. Use $\pi =$ 3.142

4. Work out the area of these circles. Use $\pi = 3.142$

(a)

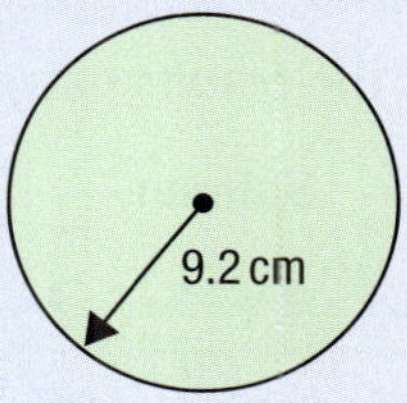

(b)

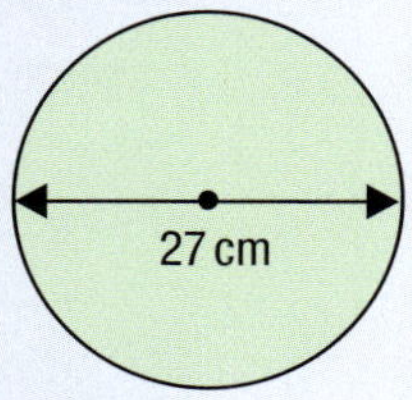

(c)

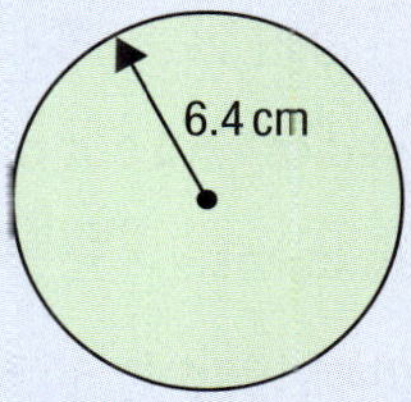

(d)

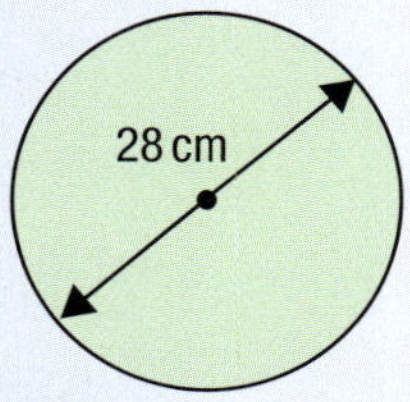

5. The diameter of a semicircle is 16 cm. Work out its area. Leave your answer in terms of π.

6. Work out the area of this shape. Use $\pi = 3.142$

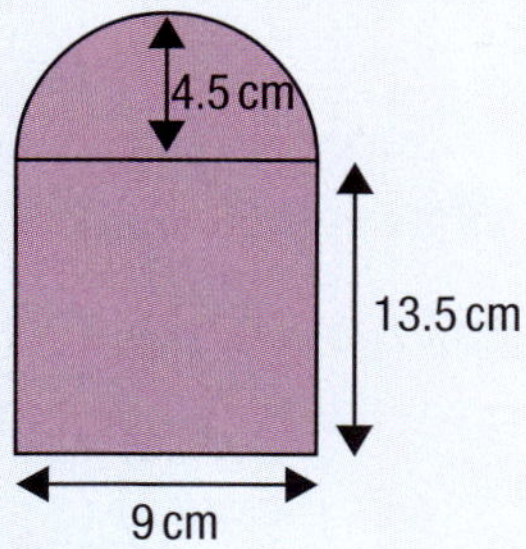

Look on the CD for more exam practice questions

21 Probability

Key facts

- All probabilities lie between 0 and 1
- An event that will definitely not happen has a **probability** of zero whilst an event that is certain to happen has a probability of 1
- Probabilities must be written as a fraction, a decimal or a percentage.
- Mutually exclusive events are events that cannot happen at the same time.
- The calculated probability of an event happening is:

  $$\text{probability of an event} = \frac{\text{number of successful outcomes}}{\text{total number of possible outcomes}}$$

  For example, if there are 4 green and 3 yellow beads in a bag and a bead is chosen at random, the probability of choosing a green bead is $\frac{4}{7}$ and the probability of choosing a yellow bead is $\frac{3}{7}$
- If the probability of an event happening is q, then the probability of it not happening is $1 - q$.
- Sample space diagrams show all the possible **outcomes** of a single event or all the possible outcomes of more than one event. For example, this sample space diagram shows the results of a spinner and a coin.

Spinner

Coin		1	2	3	4
	H	H1	H2	H3	H4
	T	T1	T2	T3	T4

- Experiments can be used to find out relative frequencies.

  $$\text{relative frequency of an event} = \frac{\text{number of times the outcome happens}}{\text{total number of trials}}$$

  The greater the number of trials in an experiment, the closer the relative frequency gets to the expected probability.

Worked example

This two-way table gives some information about the ages of students in a school.

(a) What is the probability that a student over 9 is picked at random?

(b) What is the probability that a male student under 5 is chosen at random?

	Under 5	5 to 9	Over 9	Total
Boys	20	32	23	75
Girls	14	21	30	65
Total	34	53	53	140

Solution

(a) $\frac{53}{140}$

(b) $\frac{20}{140} = \frac{1}{7}$

Definitions

- **Outcome** any possible result of an experiment
- **Probability** the chance of an event happening, given as a fraction, decimal or percentage.
Probability = (number of successful events) ÷ (total number of possible events)

Did you know?

- You have a 1 in 13 983 816 chance of getting 6 numbers on the lottery with the purchase of 1 ticket.

Look on the CD for more exam practice questions

Examiner's tips

- Probabilities need to be written as a fraction, decimal or percentage. Don't be tempted to write '6 out of 7' or '1 in 3', etc.
- If you get an answer for a probability question which is greater than 1 go back and check, since no probability answer can be greater than 1.

Can you answer these questions?

1. A bag contains 3 red, 4 blue and 6 green balls. If a ball is chosen at random from the bag what is the probability of choosing a:
   (a) red ball (b) green ball (c) pink ball?
2. The probability that I receive a letter is 42%. What is the probability that I do not receive a letter?
3. Ellen is a swimmer. The probability of her winning a race is 72%. If she swims in 50 races this season, how many races would you expect her to win?
4. Two spinners are used in a game. Spinner 1 is labelled 1, 2, 3
   Spinner 2 is labelled 2, 3, 4
   Both spinners are spun. The score is found by adding the numbers on each spinner.

		Spinner 1		
		1	2	3
Spinner 2	2	3		
	3			6
	4		6	7

   (a) Complete the table to show the possible scores.
   (b) What is the probability of an even score?
   (c) What is the probability of a score of 6?

22 Ratio and proportion

Key facts

- Ratios are used to compare two or more quantities. The quantities must be in the same unit. Ratios are written using a colon (:). For example, if there are 12 boys and 8 girls, the ratio of boys to girls is 12 : 8 which simplifies to 3 : 2 (divide both parts by 4).
- Ratios are sometimes given in the form 1 : n, where n is a number. For example, the ratio 3 : 2 can be given as 1 : $0.\dot{6}$
- Ratios can be used to share or divide quantities. When sharing a quantity in a given ratio:

  add up the total parts

  work out what one part is worth

  work out what the other parts are worth.
- Two quantities are in **proportion** if their ratio stays the same as the quantities increase or decrease. When increasing or decreasing a quantity in a given ratio:

  divide to get one part

  multiply for each new part.
- Map scales are often written as ratios, for example, 1 : 50 000

Worked examples

Example 1

Share £150 in the ratio 2 : 3

Solution 1

2 + 3 = 5 parts

1 part = $\frac{£150}{5}$ = £30

3 parts = 3 × £30 = £90

2 parts = 2 × £30 = £60

Example 2

7 pencils cost 49p. Work out the cost of 10 pencils.

Solution 2

7 pencils = 49p

1 pencil = $\frac{49\text{p}}{7}$ = 7p

therefore 10 pencils cost 10 × 7 = 70p

Definitions

- **Proportion** amounts increasing or decreasing in a given ratio are in proportion
- **Unitary method** calculating value of 1 unit, or item, them multiplying by a number of items required (used in problems of proportion and ratio)

Look on the CD for more exam practice questions

Examiner's tips

- Recipe questions appear quite often at GCSE. Remember to use the **unitary method** to find the amount needed for one person, then work out the amount needed for the new recipe.

Can you answer these questions?

1. Write each ratio in its simplest form.

   (a) 5 : 15 (b) 20 : 30 (c) 65 :13

2. In a class there are 12 girls and 15 boys.

   (a) Write down the ratio of the number of girls to the number of boys. Give your ratio in its simplest form.

   (b) Write your answer to part (a) in the form 1 : n.

3. Imran and Suki share £60 in the ratio 5 : 7

   Work out the amount that Suki receives.

4. 9 pencils cost £1.08. Work out the cost of 15 pencils.

5. (a) Poppy went on holiday to Germany. She changed £350 into Euros. The exchange rate was £1 = 1.62 Euros. Work out the number of Euros Poppy had.

   (b) Poppy came home. She had 114 Euros left. The exchange rate was £1 = 1.64 Euros. Work out how much Poppy got in pounds for 114 Euros.

23 Three-dimensional shapes

Key facts

- **3-D shapes**

Shape	Cross-section	Faces	Edges	Vertices (plural of vertex)
Cube	square	6	12	8
Cuboid	rectangle	6	12	8
Triangular prism	triangle	5	9	6
Pentagonal prism	pentagon	7	15	10
Hexagonal prism	hexagon	8	18	12

- A cylinder is a special prism with a circular **cross-section**.
- A pyramid is a 3-D shape with triangular faces meeting at a vertex. The shape of base gives number of faces and name of pyramid.

Shape	Triangular faces	Base
Triangular pyramid	4	triangle
Square pyramid	4	square

- A cone is a special pyramid whose base is a circle.
- A sphere is a 3-D shape like a ball.
- A net is a flat 2-D shape which can be cut out and folded into 3-D shape.
- Isometric grid paper is divided into equilateral triangles made from lines or dots and is useful for drawing 3-D shapes.
- Volume is the amount of space in a container and is measured in mm^3, cm^3 and m^3.

Shape	Formula for volume (word)	Formula for volume (symbol)
Cube	length × length × length	$V = l^3$
Cuboid	length × width × height	$V = lwh$
Prism	cross-section area × length	$V = a \times l$
Cylinder	base area × length	$V = \pi r^2 l$

- Surface area is the area of the net of a 3-D shape (sum of the area of all faces) and is measured in mm^2, cm^2 and m^2.
- plans and elevations

  plan is view of 3-D shape from above

  front elevation is view of 3-D shape from front

  side elevation is view of 3-D shape from side
- A plane of symmetry cuts a 3-D shape in 2 equal halves.
- 3-D coordinates locate a point using 3 axes (x, y, z).

Definitions

- **3-D shape** object with length, breadth and height
- **Cross-section** slice cut through 3-D shape parallel to its end

Did you know?

- Volume is the amount of space in a container. Capacity is the amount that will fit into a container, e.g. the amount of liquid held in a jug.

Look on the CD for more exam practice questions

Examiner's tips

- Remember to add all faces of 3-D shape when calculating surface area.
- Make sure dimensions are correct, e.g volume=length × length × length.

Can you answer these questions?

1. How many different nets can you draw for these?
   (a) cube
   (b) triangular pyramid
2. What is the volume and surface area of these?
   (a) cube (edge = 3 cm)
   (b) cuboid (l = 5 cm w = 4.5 cm h = 2.5 cm)
   (c) triangular prism (length = 10.6 cm; cross-section is right-angled triangle base 4 cm height 3 cm hypotenuse 5 cm)
3. Draw plan, side and front elevations for these.
   (a) cube (b) cuboid
   (c) triangular prism (d) sphere
4 Do these expressions represent length, area, volume or none of these?
   (a) $\pi(x^2 - y^2)$ (b) $\pi cd + 5yz$
   (c) $m + n + p$ (d) $2sbc - tsv$
   (e) $3k + 5m - \frac{1}{3}p$
5. (a) Plot these coordinates. What 2-D shape have you drawn?
   P(2, 0, 0) Q(2, 0, 3) R(2, 4, 3) S(2, 4, 0)
   (b) If another point is X(0, 0, 0), complete the solid shape by drawing 3 more points. What 3-D shape have you drawn?

24 Transformations

Have you ever wondered?

Is your face symmetrical?

Key facts

Transformation	Effects and how described
Translation	moves a shape to another position lengths and angles do not change (object and image are congruent) described by a vector
Rotation	turns a shape to another position lengths and angles do not change (object and image are congruent) described by angle, direction and centre of rotation
Reflection	reverses a shape and moves it an equal distance the other side of a mirror line lengths and angles do not change (object and image are congruent) described by the mirror line (line of symmetry)
Enlargement	moves shape to another position using scale factor angles do not change and lengths made larger or smaller by given scale factor (object and image are similar) described by scale factor and centre of enlargement

Definitions

- **Transformation** change made to the position and/or size of a shape
- **Vector** two numbers in (), used to describe translation of object; top number gives horizontal distance, bottom number gives vertical distance; up and right is positive, down and left is negative

Examiner's tips

- Describe translation giving a **vector**.
- Describe rotation giving direction, angle and centre of rotation.
- Describe reflection giving line of symmetry.
- Describe enlargement giving scale factor and centre of enlargement.

Did you know?

- Enlarge a shape by scale factor $< 1 \rightarrow$ image $<$ original
- Enlarge a shape by scale factor $= 1 \rightarrow$ image $=$ original
- Enlarge a shape by scale factor $> 1 \rightarrow$ image $>$ original

Look on the CD for more exam practice questions

Can you answer these questions?

1.

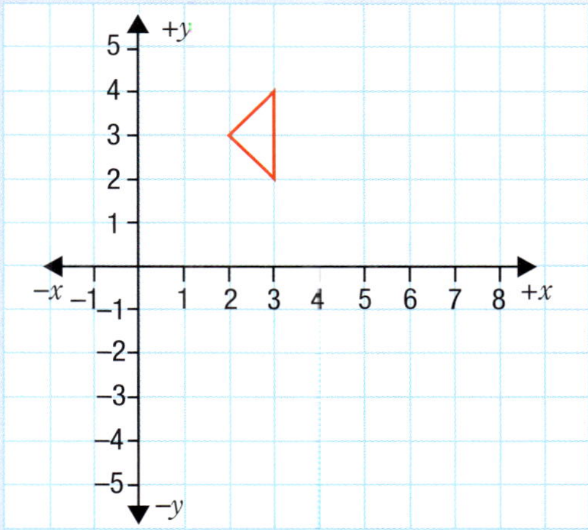

(a) Translate this shape using vector $\begin{pmatrix} 1 \\ -2 \end{pmatrix}$ to give shape A.

(b) Rotate shape A by 90° in clockwise direction about centre (4, 0) to give shape B.

(c) Reflect shape B in x-axis to give shape C.

(d) Enlarge shape C by scale factor 2 from centre (5, 2) to give D.

25 Estimating and accuracy

Have you ever wondered?

What did people use before calculators were invented?

Key facts

- When rounding, you increase or decrease a number to:

Rounding to	Number	Rounds to
Nearest integer	16.45 (nearer to 16 than 17)	16
	10.5 (nearer to 11 than 10)	11(0.5 is halfway so round up)
	9.8 (nearer to 10 than 9)	10
Nearest 10	83 (nearer to 80 than 90)	80
100	550 (nearer to 600 than 500)	600
1000	2333 (nearer to 2000 than 3000)	2000
1 significant figure(1sig.fig or sf) i.e.1st digit other than 0		
	0.00432	0.004 (2nd digit $<$ 5 so ignore)
	0.541	0.5 (2nd digit $<$ 5 so ignore)
	6.37	6 (2nd digit $<$ 5 so ignore)
	28	30* (2nd digit $>$ 5 so round up)
	179	200* (2nd digit $>$ 5 so round up)

*Remember to keep correct size of number by inserting 0 for missing digits. Not necessary for decimals.

- Estimation:

  rounds numbers to make calculation more convenient

  gives rough answer or **estimate**

  checks if answer is sensible. For example,
  $(24.6 \times 9.2) \div 2.515 \approx (25 \times 9) \div 3 = 25 \times 3 = 75$

- Calculator calculations

  $(24.6 \times 9.2) \div 2.515 = 89.988$ (same approximate size (order of magnitude) as estimate above)

  When calculating money, give answers to 2 decimal places. For example, 3.756 $\rightarrow$ £3.76

  If calculator display gives 1 decimal place, add 0 in money calculations. For example, 3.7 $\rightarrow$ £3.70

  When calculating time, remember to $\times$ 60 to change hours to minutes. For example, display shows 3.5 hours $\rightarrow$ 0.5 hours = 0.5×60 = 30 minutes $\rightarrow$ 3h 30 minutes

▶ *continued*

- **Trial and improvement**: use estimated answer to problem to try to get nearer to accurate answer. For example, the length of rectangle is 3 times its width. Its area = 192cm^2. Use trial and improvement to find the length.

Width (cm)	Length (cm)	Area (cm^2)	Comment
2	6	12	too small
4	12	48	too small
6	18	108	too small
8	24	192	correct
10	30	300	too large

- Accuracy: measurements may only be accurate within a given range. There is a minimum and maximum value.

  For example, in the rectangle above the length (24 cm) and width (8 cm) may not be exact.

  $23.5\text{ cm} \leqslant \text{length} < 24.5\text{ cm} \quad 7.5\text{ cm} \leqslant \text{width} < 8.5\text{ cm}$

Definitions

- **Estimate**
  1. approximate amount; 2. to calculate a rough answer using approximation
- **Trial and improvement** way of solving a problem by substituting values and trying to get nearer and near to the answer

Examiner's tips

- Make sure you are familiar with your calculator before you start revising.
- Read your instruction booklet.
- If your calculator uses a battery, put in a new one before the exam.

Can you answer these questions?

1. Round these to:
   (a) nearest whole number (i) 7.9 (ii) 10.1 (iii) 12.3
   (b) nearest 10 100 1000
   (i) 7.9 (10) (ii) 671 (100) (iii) 12 345 (1000)
   (c) 1 sf (i) 7.9 (ii) 101 (iii) 1234
2. Estimate these and then use a calculator to find the accurate answer.
   (a) 27×86 (b) $956 + 234$ (c) $(7.5 \times 1.4) + 4.25$
3. The square of a number is 289 Use trial and improvement to work out the number.
4. A description of a flat gives the measurement of rooms as follows.

Room	Length (m)	Width (m)
Living room	5	6
Kitchen	6	3
Bathroom	3.5	2.5
Bedroom	4	5

Rewrite the table, inserting minimum and maximum measurements.

Look on the CD for more exam practice questions

26 Constructions and loci

Key facts

- Constructions: use straight edge (e.g. ruler) and compasses.

Construction	Instructions
Equilateral triangle	(i) draw line AB (ii) open compasses to length AB, compass point on A, draw arc above line (iii) repeat with compass point on B (iv) arcs cross at C (v) join A, B, C to form equilateral triangle ABC *check that AB = BC = CA
Perpendicular bisector of straight line	(i) draw line AB (ii) open compasses to more than half length AB, compass point on A, draw arc from above to below line (iii) repeat with compass point on B (iv) arcs cross at C and D (v) join C and D to form perpendicular bisector of AB *check that CD is at right angles to AB
Bisector of ∠ABC	(i) open compasses to less than half length AB (ii) compass point on A, draw arc to cross AB at D and AC at E (iii) with same length and compass point on D and then E, draw arcs between AB and AC to cross at F (iv) join A and F to form bisector of ∠ABC *check that ∠CAF = ∠BAF

- Locus (pl. loci) point that moves according to a given rule.

Locus	Description
given distance from a fixed point	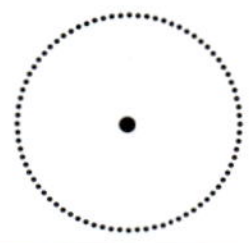
given distance from a fixed line	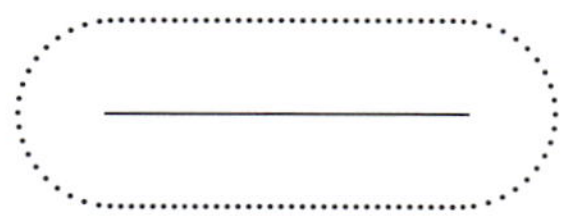
equidistant from 2 fixed points	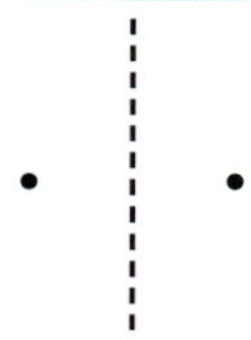
equidistant from 2 fixed lines	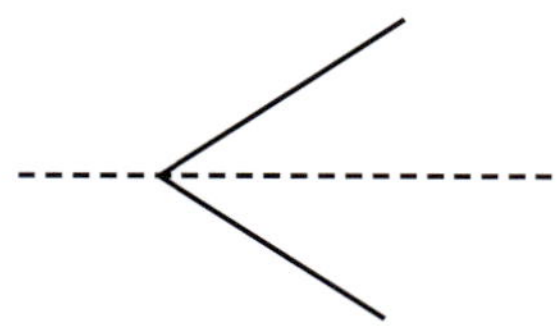
combined loci	follows more than 1 set of rules and locus is where paths cross over

- **Regions:** points may lie in given area or region rather than on line.

Definitions

- **Equidistant** point is equidistant from 2 or more points, or lines, if it is the same distance from each of them
- **Region** area satisfying given conditions

Did you know?

- Locus is Latin for place.

Look on the CD for more exam practice questions

Examiner's tips

- Check all drawing equipment before the exam. Sharpen pencils, including your compass pencil.
- When drawing a locus, imagine you are actually walking that path.
- Don't forget to include a scale for constructions.
- You should not rub out construction marks, e.g. arcs on your drawing. They show your working method.

Can you answer these questions?

1. Construct these using a straight edge and compasses.
   (a) equilateral triangle PQR of side 4 cm and measure ∠PQR.
   (b) perpendicular bisector of PQ, crossing PQ at M and measure PM.
   (c) bisector of ∠RPQ, crossing RQ at N and measure ∠RPN.
2. Construct the locus of the path walked by these.
   (a) goat attached by a taut rope, length 2 m, to a vertical pole in a field.
   (b) cat walking at fixed distance of 1.25 m from a hedge.
3. A shopping mall is built in the shape of an equilateral triangle. The vertices each have a department store (X, Y, Z). Draw the locus of a path walked by a boy:
   (a) equidistant from XY and XZ
   (b) equidistant from X and Y.
   (c) A woman walks in the same shopping mall so that she is always nearer to XZ than XY. Shade the region that obeys this rule.
4. A dog buries a bone in a garden (5 m × 8 m) so that it is 6 m from L and equidistant from KN and NM.

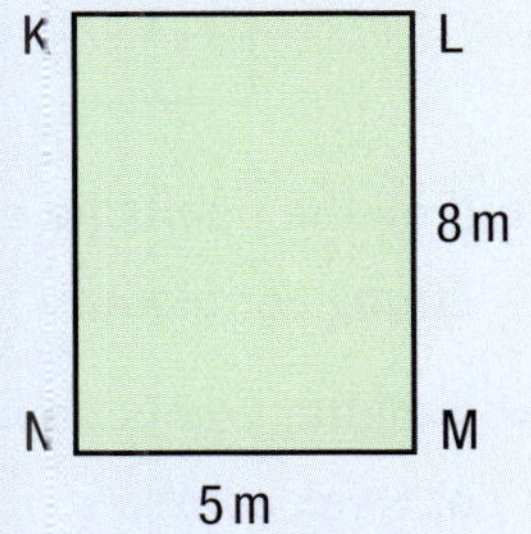

Construct the locus for each rule and mark the position of the bone with B.

27 Scatter graphs

Key facts

- Scatter graphs illustrate the relationship between 2 quantities. Crosses are usually used for points.
- **Line of best fit** is drawn through estimated middle of points.
- Another word for relationship is **correlation**. This can be:

positive correlation

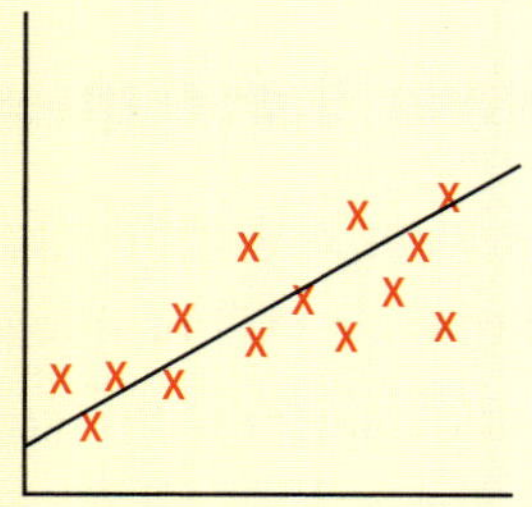

negative correlation

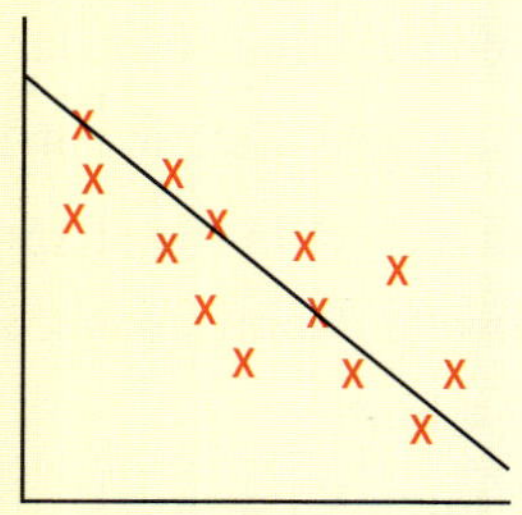

zero correlation

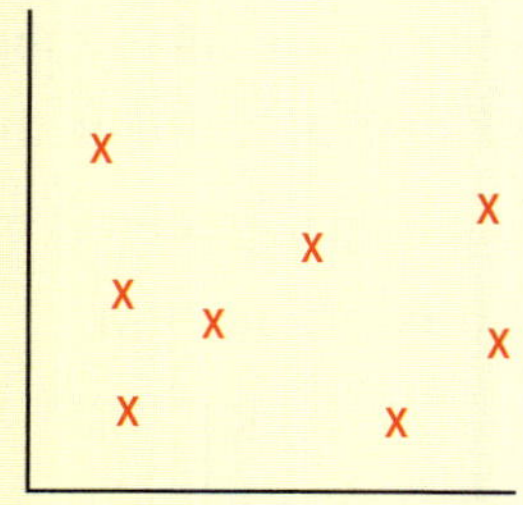

- If all the points lie close to the line of best fit, there is said to be high or strong correlation.
- If all the points do not lie close to the line of best fit, there is said to be low or weak correlation.

Definitions

- **Line of best fit**
  line drawn approximately through the middle of points of a scatter graph
- **Correlation**
  connection between 2 variables

Examiner's tips

- Always use a sharp pencil to draw scatter graph points and line of best fit. This gives greater accuracy.
- Never use a pen to draw a graph, you may need to adjust your drawing.

Can you answer these questions?

1. Draw a scatter graph to illustrate the relationship between the age of a car and its mileage as shown in this table.

Year	Mileage
1	10 000
2	17 000
3	26 000
4	34 000
5	46 000
6	52 000
7	64 000
8	70 000

2. Draw a line of best fit on your scatter graph. What correlation is there?
3. Describe the correlation between each of these.
   (a) height and weight
   (b) height and shoe size
   (c) temperature and sale of ice creams
   (d) age of car and its value
   (e) temperature and shoe size
   (f) distance travelled by car and petrol in tank

Look on the CD for more exam practice questions

28 Pythagoras' theorem

Key facts

- The **hypotenuse** is the longest side of a right angled triangle. It is always opposite the right angle.
- **Pythagoras' theorem** states that:

  in any right angled triangle the square on the hypotenuse is equal to the sum of the squares on the other two sides.

  Using the letters in the diagram, the theorem is written as:

  $c^2 = a^2 + b^2$

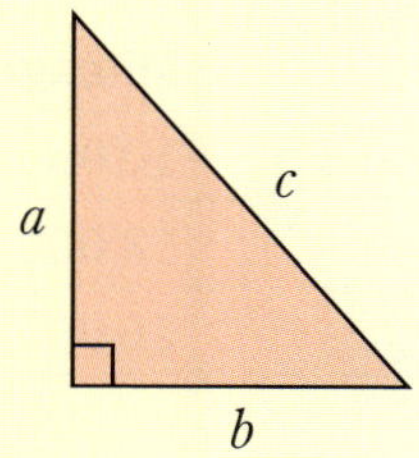

  $c^2 = a^2 + b^2$ is used to calculate the hypotenuse.

  $a^2 = c^2 - b^2$ is used to calculate one of the shorter sides.

- Pythagoras' theorem can be used to find the length of a line joining two points.

Worked example

Work out the length of the line AB.

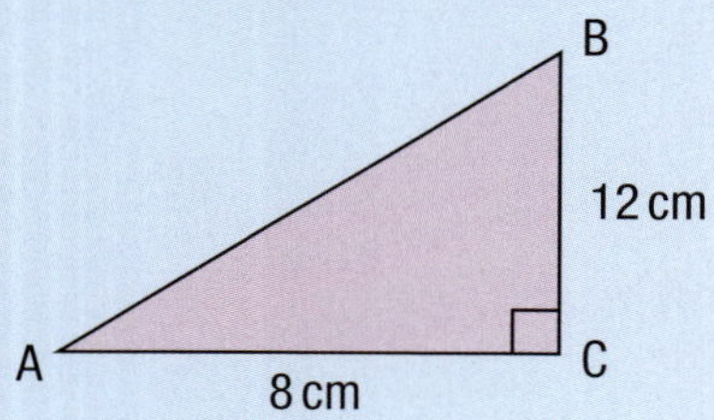

Solution

As you are given the lengths of the other two sides of the right-angled triangle, you can use Pythagoras' theorem to find the length of AB.

Pythagoras' theorem states:

$$c^2 = b^2 + c^2$$

where c is the length of the longest side (or the hypotenuse), and a and b are the lengths of the other two sides.

Using Pythagoras' theorem to find the length of AB

$$c^2 = 8^2 + 12^2$$
$$= 64 + 144$$
$$= 208$$

Using the square root button on your calculator

$$c = \sqrt{208}$$
$$= 14.4 \text{ cm (3sf)}$$

So the length of the line AB is 14.4 cm

Examiner's tips

- When answering a question, decide carefully which formula to use.
- Write down the formula $c^2 = a^2 + b^2$ and then substitute the correct numbers.
- Remember to square root the answer you obtain at the end, in order to get the length.

Definitions

- **Hypotenuse** longest side in a right-angled triangle
- **Pythagoras' theorem** in a right-angled triangle, the square of the hypotenuse is equal to the sum of the squares of the other two sides

Look on the CD for more exam practice questions

Can you answer these questions?

1. Work out the lengths of the sides marked with letters in these triangles.
   Give your answer to 2 decimal places where appropriate.

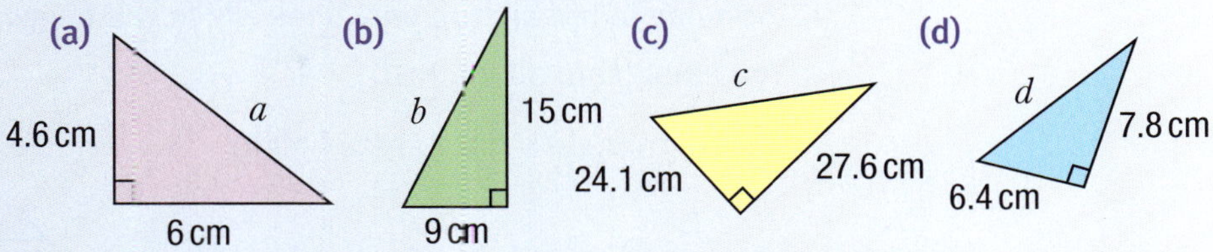

2. Work out the lengths of the sides marked with letters in these triangles.
   Give your answer to 2 decimal places where appropriate.

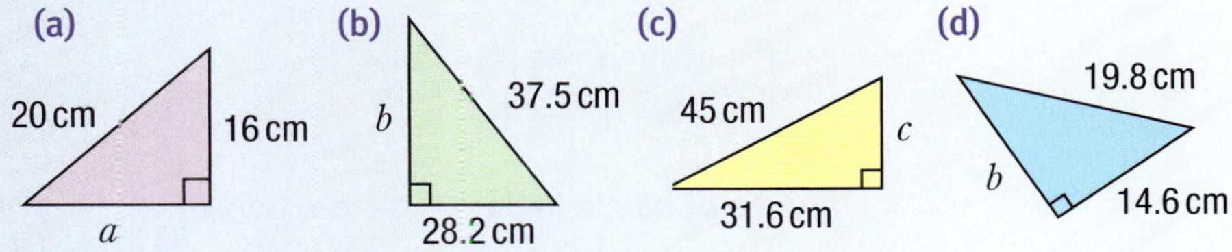

3. Find the length of the line joining B(4, 6) and C(7, 10).

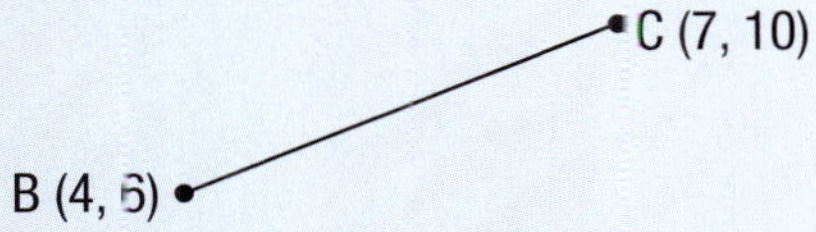

4. (a) Work out the length of the side marked x in the triangle. Give your answer correct to 2 decimal places.
   (b) Work out the perimeter of the triangle. Give your answer correct to 2 decimal places.

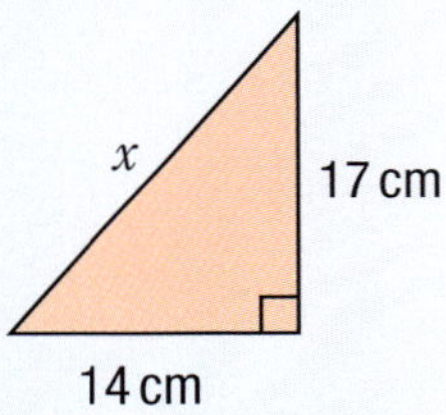

5. Work out the area of the triangle.
   Give your answer correct to 1 decimal place

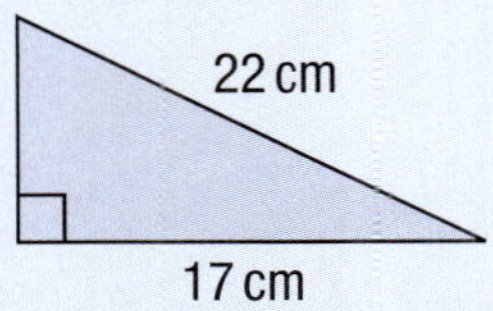

6. Calculate the length of the diagonal of this rectangle, giving your answer correct to 1 decimal place.

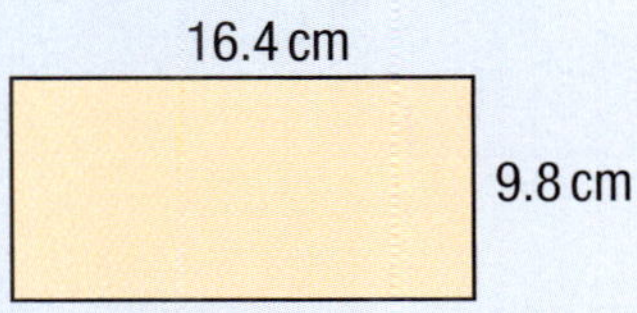

Essential formulae

A comprehensive list of formulae you will need to know is given below. The formulae in red are the only ones which will be given on the formulae sheet. You must learn all the rest.

Area of triangle $= \frac{1}{2} \times$ base $\times$ height

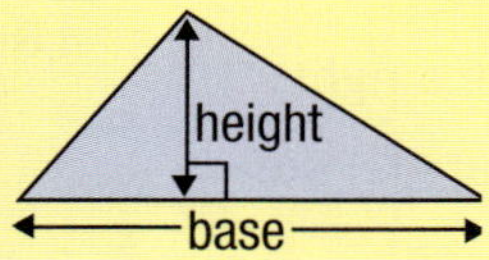

Circumference of circle $= \pi \times$ diameter

$= 2 \times \pi \times$ radius

Area of circle $= \pi \times (\text{radius})^2$

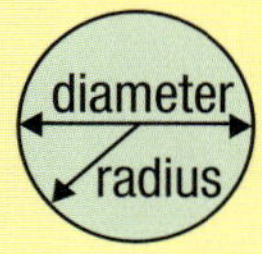

Area of parallelogram = base $\times$ height

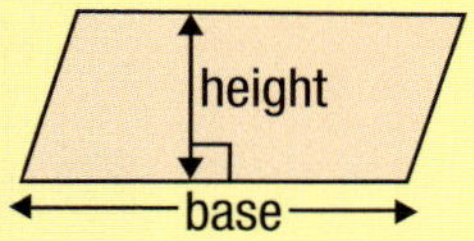

Area of trapezium $= \frac{1}{2}(a + b)h$

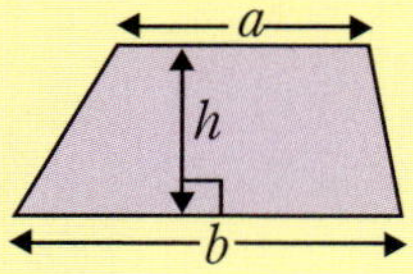

Volume of cuboid = length $\times$ width $\times$ height

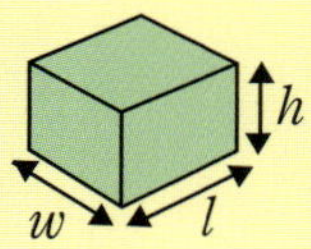

Volume of cylinder $= \pi r^2 h$

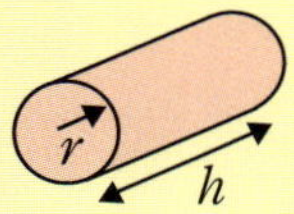

Volume of prism = (area of cross-section) $\times$ length

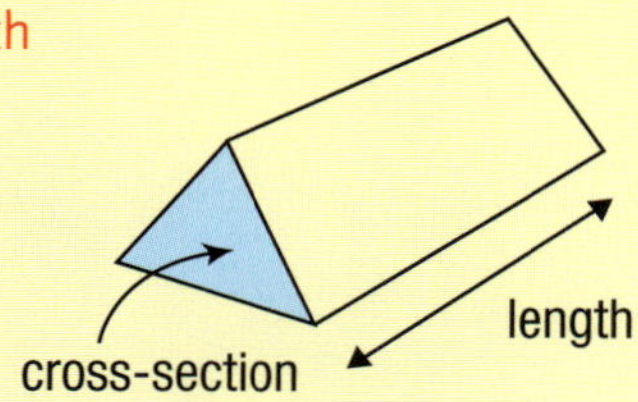

Pythagoras' theorem $a^2 + b^2 = c^2$

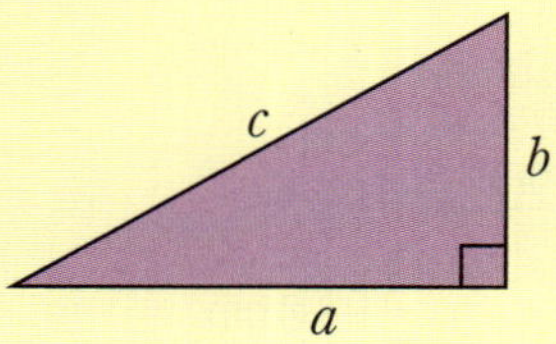

speed $= \frac{\text{distance}}{\text{time}}$ time $= \frac{\text{distance}}{\text{speed}}$ distance = speed $\times$ time

density $= \frac{\text{mass}}{\text{volume}}$

Glossary

Topic	Word	Definition
1	**sum**	total of 2 or more numbers
1	**difference**	subtraction of a small number from a larger number
1	**product**	result of multiplying 2 or more numbers together
2	**database**	large amount of information stored in an organised way
2	**frequency**	number of observations or events happening
3.1	**parallel**	parallel lines always stay the same distance apart and never meet
3.1	**perpendicular**	a line at right angles to another line
3.2	**polygon**	2-D shape with many straight sides
3.2	**bearing**	direction of an object, given by 3-figure angle, measured clockwise from the north line
4	**numerator**	number above the line in a fraction
4	**denominator**	number below the line in a fraction
5	**2-D**	two-dimensional – has length and breadth but no depth
5	**symmetry**	stays the same when reflected or rotated
7	**significant figures**	digits, counting from the left, needed to give a number the correct degree of accuracy
8	**algebra**	part of mathematics using letters for unknown numbers and variables
8	**expression**	a statement which can have letters and numbers or both
8	**factorising**	to break up, or separate, into factors
9, 20	**perimeter**	the boundary or edge of an enclosed area, as well as the length of that boundary
9	**area**	measure, in square units, e.g. mm^2, cm^2, m^2, of the surface of a shape or object
10	**square numbers**	numbers raised to the power of 2; product of 2 equal factors
10	**cube numbers**	numbers raised to power of 3; product of 3 equal factors
12	**improper fraction**	fraction with numerator greater than its denominator
12	**mixed number**	includes both a whole number and fractional part
14	**speed**	distance travelled per unit time
14	**density**	mass per unit volume of an object
15	**depreciate**	decrease in value
16	**average**	normal or standard amount or value

16	**range**	difference between greatest and least values of data
17	**integer**	any whole number, positive or negative, including zero
18	**index**	small digit to the right of a number, or letter, giving the number of times it is multiplied by itself
19	**expression**	statement with letters or numbers or both
21	**outcome**	any possible result of an experiment
21	**probability**	the chance of an event happening, given as a fraction, decimal or percentage. probability=(number of successful events)÷(total number of possible events)
22	**proportion**	amounts increasing or decreasing in a given ratio are in proportion
22	**unitary method**	calculating value of 1 unit, or item, then multiplying by number of items required (used in problems of proportion and ratio)
23	**3-D shape**	object with length, breadth and height
23	**cross-section**	slice cut through 3-D shape parallel to its end
24	**transformation**	change made to the position and/or size of a shape
24	**vector**	2 numbers in ( ), used to describe translation of object; top number gives horizontal distance, bottom number gives vertical distance; up and right is positive, down and left is negative
25	**estimate**	1. approximate amount; 2. to calculate a rough answer using approximation
25	**trial and improvement**	way of solving a problem by substituting values and trying to get nearer and nearer to the answer
26	**equidistant**	point is equidistant from 2 or more points, or lines, if it is the same distance from each of them
26	**region**	area satisfying given conditions
27	**line of best fit**	line drawn approximately through middle of points of a scatter graph
27	**correlation**	connection between 2 variables
28	**hypotenuse**	longest side in a right-angled triangle
28	**Pythagoras' theorem**	in a right-angled triangle, the square of the hypotenuse is equal to the sum of the squares of the other two sides

Answers

1 Introducing number (page 9)

1. 12 64 67 72 209 5462 6384
2. (a) 2740 (b) 62 500
3. 138
4. £6.50
5. (a) 7 14 21 28
   (b) 12 24 36 48
   (c) 4 8 12 16
6. (a) 1 2 4 8
   (b) 1 2 3 4 6 12
   (c) 1 2 4 7 14 28
7. (a) HCF = 3 LCM = 60
   (b) HCF = 2 LCM = 30
   (c) HCF = 4 LCM = 12

2 Collecting and recording data (page 11)

3. (a) continuous (b) discrete
   (c) continuous (d) discrete
4 (a) should have age group response boxes
   (b) is open-ended (c) is biased

3 Angles 1 and 2 (page 13)

Angles 1 (page 13)

1. (a) 35° (b) 75°
   (c) 120° (d) 300°
2. (a) obtuse (b) reflex
   (c) right angle (d) acute
3. (a) a = 18° (b) b = 100°
   (c) c = 55° (d) d = 120°
   (e) e = 293° (f) f = 54°
   g = h = i = 126°

Angles 2 (page 16)

1. (a) a = 55° b = 75°
   (b) a = b = c = 60° d = 120°
   (c) a = b = 65° c = 115°
   (d) a = 42° b = 132°
2. (a) 65° (b) 150°
   (c) 130° (d) d = 135° e = 45°
   (e) e = 130° f = 40°
3. (a) 70° (b) 125° (c) 85°
4. (a) 135° (b) 15° (c) 245°

4 Fractions and decimals 1 (page 19)

1. $\frac{40}{64} = \frac{5}{8}$
2. (a) $\frac{2}{3} = \frac{6}{9}$ (b) $\frac{6}{7} = \frac{18}{21}$ (c) $\frac{10}{15} = \frac{2}{3}$
3. $\frac{1}{6}$ $\frac{5}{24}$ $\frac{7}{12}$
4. 3 hundredths.
5. 6.05 6.4 6.57 6.572 6.72
6. $2\frac{69}{100}$
7. $0.\dot{2}$

5 Two-dimensional shapes (page 21)

1. A: line B: line P: none S: rotational
2. (a) 60° (b) 108°
3. circles, hexagons, triangles
4.

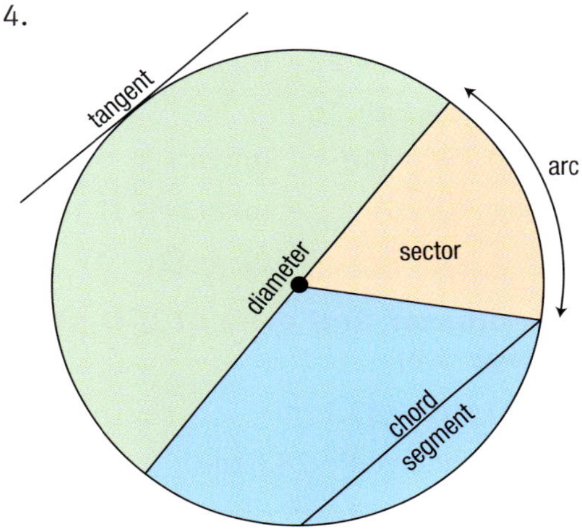

6 Directed numbers (page 23)

1. −10 °C −6 °C −2 °C 0 °C 4 °C 7 °C
2. −2 °C
3. (a) −5 (b) −3 (c) −5 (d) −1
   (e) −1 (f) −8
4. (a) −8 (b) 12 (c) −6 (d) 3
   (e) −20 (f) 24
5. 0.5

7 Decimals 2 (page 25)

1. (a) 9.67 (b) 11.34
   (c) 110 (d) 69.4
   (e) 0.2763 (f) 0.0484

(g) 74 620 (h) 2.187

(i) 1.72

2. (a) 24.3 (b) 4.8

(c) 6100 (d) 85

(e) 1600 (f) 9

3. (a) 6.5 (b) 12.4

(c) 4.5 (d) 16.9

4. (a) 4000 (b) 80

(c) 2000 (d) 200

5. £255.50

8 Algebra (page 27)

1. $x + y$

2. (a) 7 (b) 5

(c) 17 (d) 8

(e) 5

3. (a) $5a$ (b) $5a + 6b$

(c) $4c - d$

4. (a) $3n - 3$ (b) $2n + 8$

(c) $2a^2 + a$ (d) $3b^2 - ab$

(e) $n^2 + 3n + 2$ (f) $n^2 - 4n + 3$

(g) $n^2 - 8n + 16$

5. (a) $13c + 11d$ (b) $2n + 3$

6. (a) $5(a + 2)$ (b) $8(2a - 1)$

(c) $y(2 - 3x)$ (d) $4y\,(2y - 1)$

9 Perimeter and area of 2-D shapes (page 29)

1. (a) area = 33.1 cm^2

perimeter = 28.6 cm

(b) area = 48 cm^2 perimeter = 32 cm

2. (a) 32 cm^2 (b) 1102.7 m^2

3. (a) 23.6 cm^2 (b) 30 cm^2

(c) 18.8 cm^2 (d) 57.6 cm^2

4. (a) 4 cm^2 (b) 64 000 000 m^2

(c) 25 000 000 mm^2

(d) 1 km^2

10 Sequences (page 31)

1 (a) 36, 30

(b) Subtract 6 each time.

2. (a) Add 4 each time.

(b)

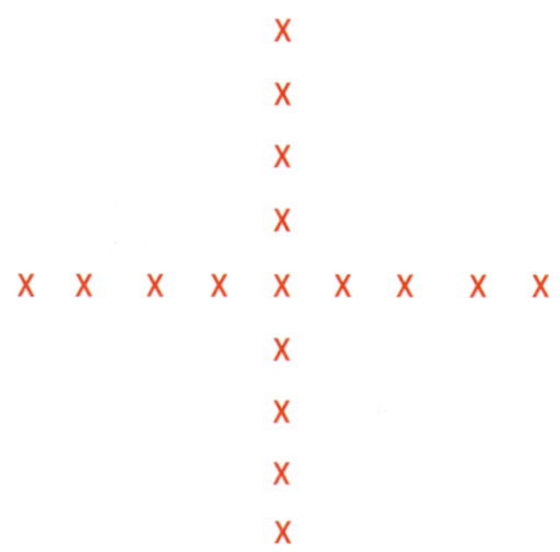

pattern 5

(c)

Pattern number	1	2	3	4	5	6
Number of crosses	1	5	9	**13**	**17**	**21**

3. (a) $2n$ (b) $5n - 1$

(c) $3n + 2$

11 Graphs (page 34)

1. (a) A = (2, 3) B = (0, −4) C = (−4, 2)

D = (4, −3) E = (−2, −3)

(b) (3, 0)

2. (a)

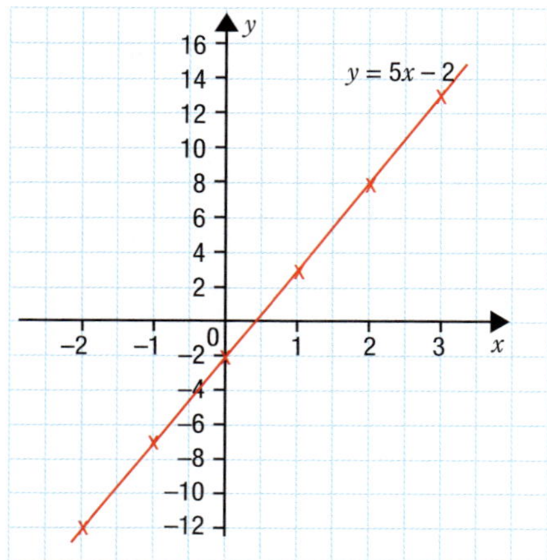

(b) $k = 1.8$

3 (a) (i) gradient = 5 (ii) y-intercept = 1

(b) (i) gradient = −4 (ii) y-intercept = 2

12 Fractions 2 (page 36)

1. (a) 6 (b) 18

2. 340

3. (a) $\frac{35}{60} = \frac{7}{12}$ (b) $\frac{18}{24} = \frac{3}{4}$

4. (a) $1\frac{1}{6}$ (b) $\frac{8}{21}$ (c) $6\frac{3}{35}$

5. (a) $\frac{5}{6}$ (b) $\frac{1}{14}$ (c) $\frac{27}{65}$

6. (a) $\frac{9}{10}$ (b) $2\frac{2}{11}$ (c) $2\frac{9}{28}$

13 Processing, representing and interpreting data (page 38)

1.

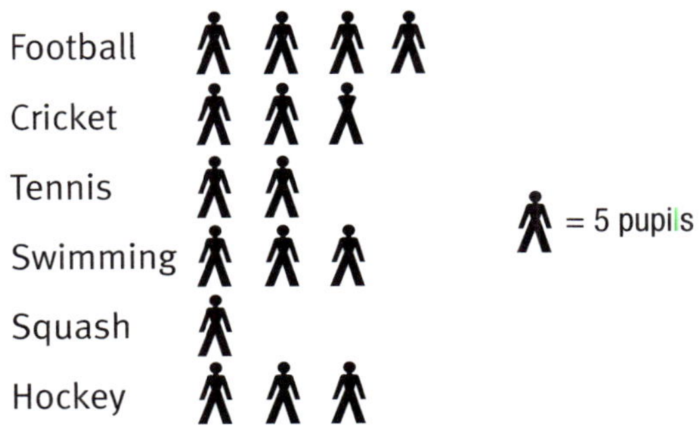

2.

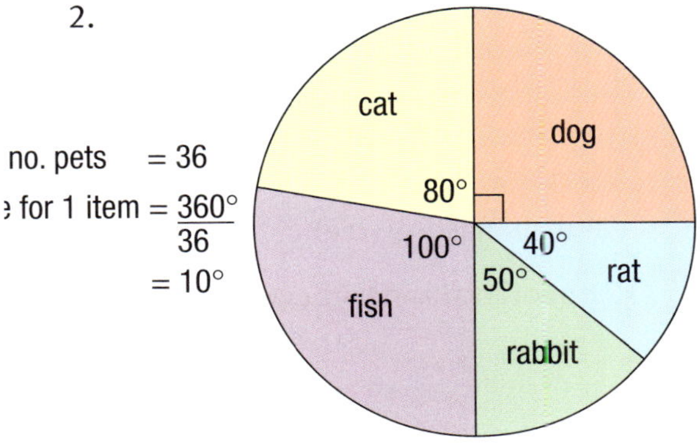

3. (a) June (b) 100
 (c) 1385

4.

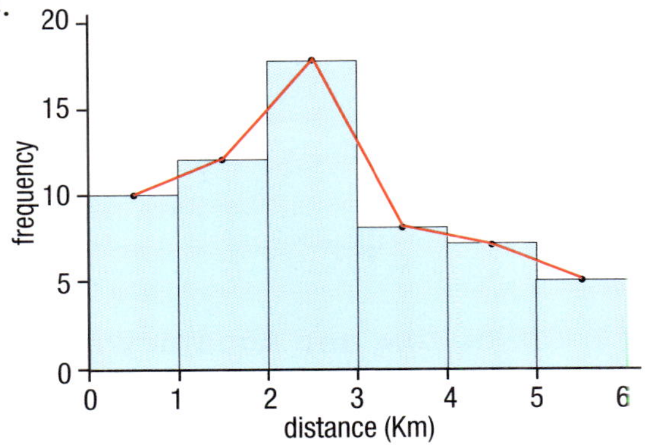

14 Measure (page 41)

1. (a) 22 °C (b) 0.4 kg
 (c) 240 g (d) 45litres
2. (a) 1135 (b) 0005
 (c) 1956
3. (a) 9.10pm (b) 2.35am
 (c) 12.15pm
4. (a) 44 minutes (b) 1131(34 minutes)
 (c) (i) 1158 (ii) 1220
5. (a) 15.5 cm (b) 2600 m
 (c) 150 000 cm (d) 3 km
6. (a) 2h 51minutes (b) 10 km
 (c) 980 g/l

15 Percentages (page 43)

1. (a) (i) $\frac{31}{50}$ (ii) 0.62
 (b) (i) $\frac{9}{20}$ (ii) 0.45
 (c) (i) $\frac{79}{100}$ (ii) 0.79
2. 0.4 $\frac{9}{20}$ 48% $\frac{5}{8}$
3. (a) 22.2 kg (b) £2295
4. £552.50
5. £676
6. 22.5%
7. 56.7%

16 Averages and ranges (page 45)

1. (a) 133 cm 133 cm 133 cm 14 cm
 (b) 155.4 cm 156 cm 156 cm 10 cm
 (c) 174 cm 21 cm
2. 10 swimming athletics
3. X more successful (mode $X = 26$
 mode $Y = 21$ range $X = 43$
 range $Y = 42$)
4. (a) $120 \leqslant w < 130$ (b) 60 g
 (c) 130.2 g

17 Equations and inequalities (page 47)

1 (a) $n = 16$ (b) $n = 6$ (c) $n = 18$
 (d) $n = 3$ (e) $n = -2$ (f) $n = -\frac{1}{2}$
2. (a) $n = 7$ (b) $n = 2$ (c) $n = 2$
3. (a) $x = 1.5$ (b) $x = 3$ (c) $x = 3.5$
 (d) $x = 4$ (e) $x = \frac{4}{3}$ or $x = 1\frac{1}{3}$
 (f) $x = \frac{9}{5}$ or $x = 1\frac{4}{5}$
4. $x = 3$
5. (a)

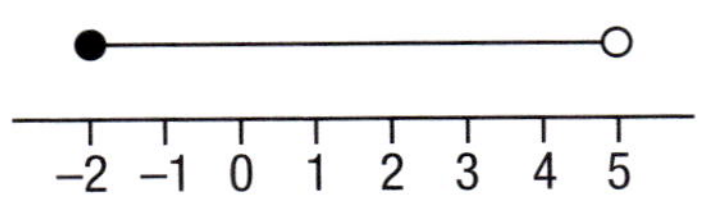

 (b) –2 –1 0 1 2 3 4
6. (a) $n < 4$ (b) $n < 3$ (c) $x \leq 1$

18 Powers and roots (page 49)

1. (a) 4^5 (b) 3^6
2 (a) 125 (b) 1296 (c) 64 (d) 17
3. (a) ±9 (b) 5 (c) 3 (d) ±12
4. (a) 24 (b) 13 (c) 22
5. (a) 5^9 (b) 5^3 (c) 5^2 (d) 5^7

19 Formulae (page 51)

1. £216
2. $\frac{\text{sweets in a packet}}{5}$ = number of sweets each person receives
3. $v = 36$
4. $C = 20x + 90y$
5. $c = \frac{a - d}{b}$
6. $\frac{p - a^2b}{2} = c$

20 Circumference and area of a circle (page 53)

1. (a) 37.704 cm (b) 43.988 cm
   (c) 47.13 cm (d) 38.961 cm
2. 3.91 cm
3. 51.42 cm
4. (a) 265.94 cm^2 (b) 572.63 cm^2
   (c) 128.70 cm^2 (d) 615.83 cm^2
5. $32\pi\ cm^2$
6. 153.31 cm^2

21 Probability (page 55)

1 (a) $\frac{3}{13}$ (b) $\frac{6}{13}$ (c) 0
2. 58%
3. 36 races
4. (a)

		Spinner 1		
		1	**2**	**3**
Spinner 2	**2**	3	4	5
	3	4	5	6
	4	5	6	7

(b) $\frac{4}{9}$

(c) $\frac{2}{9}$

22 Ratio and proportion (page 57)

1. (a) 1 : 3 (b) 2 :3 (c) 5 : 1
2. (a) 4 : 5 (b) 1 : 1.25
3. £35
4. £1.80
5. (a) 567 Euros (b) £69.51

23 Three-dimensional shapes (page 59)

1. (a) 11 (b) 2
2. (a) 27 cm^3 54 cm^2
   (b) 56.25 cm^3 92.5 cm^2
   (c) 63.6 cm^3 139.2 cm^2
3.

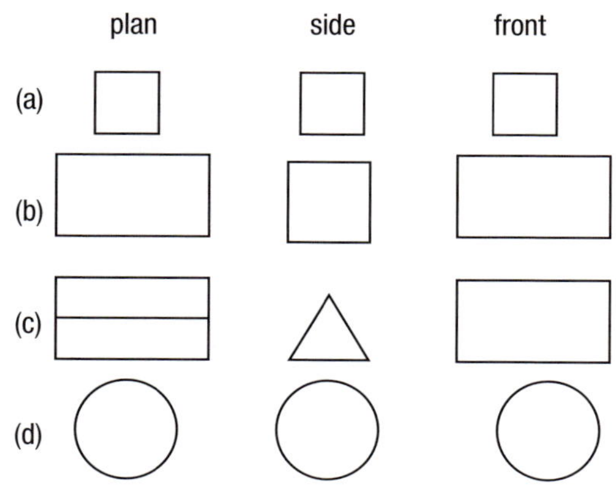

4. (a) area (b) area
   (c) length (d) volume
   (e) length
5. (a) rectangle (b) cuboid

24 Transformations (page 61)

1.

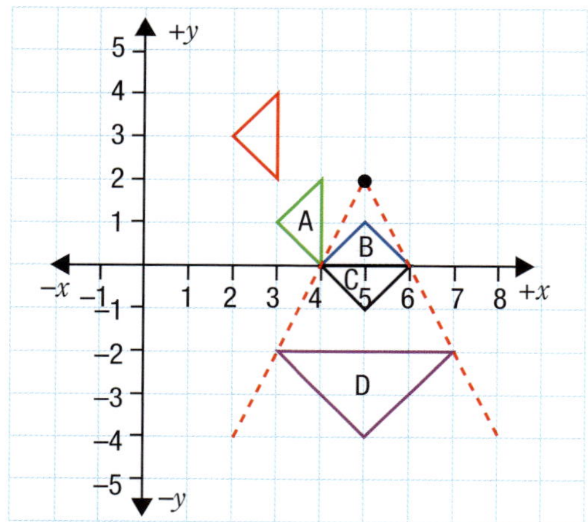

25 Estimating and accuracy (page 63)

1. (a) (i) 8 (ii) 10 (iii) 12
   (b) (i) 10 (ii) 700 (iii) 12 000
   (c) (i) 8 (ii) 100 (iii) 1000
2. (a) 2700 2322 (b) 1190 = (960 + 230)
   (c) 12 14.75
3. 17
4.

Room	Length (m)	Width(m)
Living room	$4.5 \leqslant 5 < 5.5$	$5.5 \leqslant 6 < 6.5$
Kitchen	$5.5 \leqslant 6 < 6.5$	$2.5 \leqslant 3 < 3.5$
Bathroom	$3.45 \leqslant 3.5 < 3.55$	$2.45 \leqslant 2.5 < 2.55$
Bedroom	$3.5 \leqslant 4 < 4.5$	$4.5 \leqslant 5 < 5.5$

26 Constructions and loci (page 65)

1. (a) 60°   (b) 2 cm   (c) 30°

2. (a)

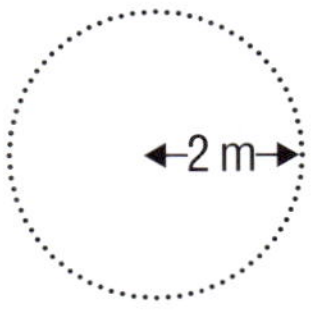

(b)

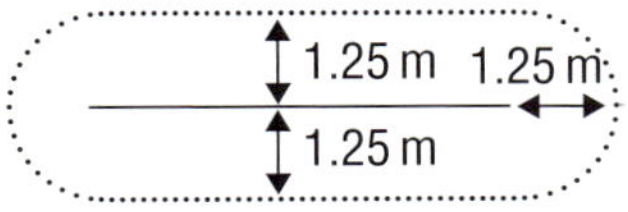

3.

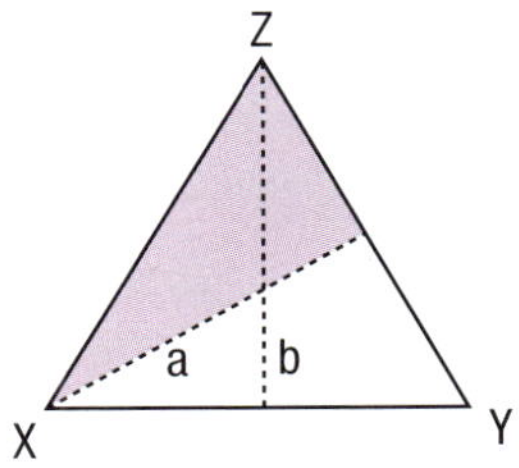

4.

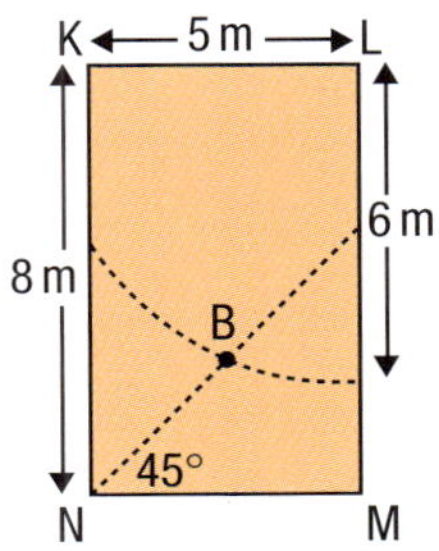

27 Scatter graphs (page 67)

1.

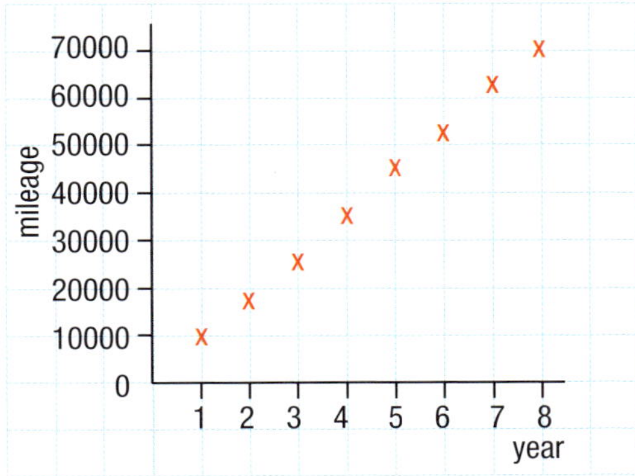

2. positive

3. (a) positive   (b) positive
   (c) positive   (d) negative
   (e) zero   (f) negative

28 Pythagoras' theorem (page 69)

1. (a) $a = 7.56$ cm   (b) $b = 17.49$ cm
   (c) $c = 36.64$ cm   (d) $d = 10.09$ cm

2. (a) $a = 12$ cm   (b) $b = 24.72$ cm
   (c) $c = 32.04$ cm   (d) $d = 13.37$cm

3. 5 units

4. (a) $x = 22.02$ cm   (b) perimeter = 53.02 cm

5. Area = 118.7 cm^2

6. 19.1 cm